A RICH
FUTURE

A RICH FUTURE

ESSENTIAL FINANCIAL CONCEPTS FOR YOUTH

NOAH BOOTH

Contact: arichfuture@gmail.com

ISBN 978-1-7779275-0-9 (softcover)
ISBN 978-1-7779275-1-6 (ePub)
ISBN 978-1-7779275-2-3 (Audio book)

Project management by Heidy Lawrance, WeMakeBooks.ca
Text design and print production by Beth Crane, WeMakeBooks.ca
Cover design by Kim Monteforte, kimmontefortedesign.com
Edited by Alexa Dupuis-Bissonnette of Dupuis Editing and Andrea Lemieux
Author photo by Celeste Booth

Disclaimer: The views and opinions expressed in this publication are for your general interest and should not be relied on as financial or legal advice. Everyone's situation is different, and not all investment strategies or products discussed may be appropriate for you.

Printed and bound in Canada

CONTENTS

Chapter Seven — Advanced Lessons   117

Epilogue   127

Glossary   129

Notes   135

AUTHOR'S NOTE

You may not know a lot about finances. Many people don't, but the good news is that this is more than OK. Do not worry if you have come into trouble with debt, spending, saving, or anything else related to finances. Growing up in an age of social media and targeted marketing towards young people like you and me is the difficult reality that we face. Companies spend literally millions upon millions of dollars trying to get you to part with your money, and unfortunately they are very successful in doing so. You need to remember that it's *not* your fault if you have run into financial difficulties. Some, and maybe most, of the information in this book may be new to you. This is good as it means you are learning. Please remember that we are in this together and this book is to help you.

ACKNOWLEDGEMENTS

Without the help of so many people, this book would never have been possible. From friends to family to teachers—I thank everyone who gave me their advice, time, and help. In particular, I thank the following for guiding and helping me in the making of this book: My grandparents, whom I thank so much for inspiring me and guiding me from the day I was born. My Grandpa for being so supportive, saving me thousands of dollars in legal advice, and providing excellent business strategy. Nana and Papa for teaching me so many valuable financial lessons and encouraging me along the way. Carol for the invaluable connections and advice. My teacher, Mike Byers, who first prompted this book idea back in eighth grade, and for the amazing reference letters that helped me get to where I am today. David Chilton for the generous phone calls loaded full of precious advice, and access to his excellent online course on self-publishing. Lexi Dupuis, my first editor for enthusiastically tearing my work apart and making it better in every way. Ryan Lynch, for generously offering me never-ending support and advice. A special thanks to Tony Maiorino for taking the chance on a young kid. Ken Grewal and Sloane Keilty for very insightful input. My coaches and high school teachers, who showed me great support in this endeavor. My siblings for tolerating the use of their names in this book. Sheila Doyle for the last-minute wise advice. Marie Ingram for the great advice and help solving problems. My second editor, Andrea Lemieux, for bearing with me, enhancing my book, and teaching me many lessons in writing. Heidy Lawrance of WeMakeBooks.ca for managing the production of this book, and Beth Crane for the awesome design work. And finally, Mom and Dad for all of the love, support, ideas, and dedication to the fullest for everything that I do.

INTRODUCTION

You may be wondering what kind of teenager would want to write a book about personal finance and investing. Really, I'm just a pretty normal kid. I love sports (running, soccer, basketball, skiing, sailing, competitive swimming, surfing, and triathlons), school's okay, and 1 like to hang out with my friends. My main sport is running; however I also swim competitively and play basketball. I'm a long-distance runner (sadly, not a sprinter—that would be so much easier), and I hope to pursue elite running through university and later in life. In the summer 1 like to sail and windsurf. I also do a three-week canoe trip in northern Canada each summer with a great wilderness program.

Back to the financial side of my life. Since a young age I've had an interest in earning, saving, and investing money. I've been fortunate enough to have many people in my inner circle who have guided me and taught me lessons that I found many teenagers don't ever get taught in school or at home. With the lack of financial education that many people are getting, I thought to myself, why not share these lessons and help all of those other kids out there, and *hopefully* make some money by doing it! I was inspired by reading *The Wealthy Barber* at a young age, which made me start looking for creative ways to earn, save, and invest my money. I decided that one of the best ways to encompass all of my ideas, experiences, and lessons was to write a book geared for teens. With my own experiences, help from others with more expertise, lots of research (and some guidance from my parents and grandparents) I set out to write the book that you are now holding in your hands. I hope you enjoy it, and learn a thing or two.

Okay, to be reading this right now you must be in search of financial wellbeing. Or, maybe you don't really care, and it was your parents' idea to buy this book for you and you had to go along with it. Well, now you're reading it, so you might as well give it a shot. Because this book is full of real-world advice—from the viewpoint of an actual teenager—and it's easy to read and contains simple (but really important!) material, it is sure to set you up for life, helping you to achieve your financial goals.

This book covers a wide variety of topics informed by advice and lessons from actual experts, but from the viewpoint of an actual teenager. By the end of reading this book, you will have the knowledge and ability to set yourself up to have a successful and healthy financial future.

In my experience, this stuff just isn't being taught enough. In school there are very few financial literacy courses, and when there are they aren't usually mandatory. There is a knowledge gap among kids in the world, some have access to information from parents, school, and other forms of financial literacy education while others do not. It doesn't take an expert to realize that if a kid isn't having any discussions about money with the adults in their lives or at school, they are probably not going to know a whole lot. I'm not sure how they (the government, teachers, and adults in general) expect the future generations of young Canadians to be financially secure and independent if this kind of stuff isn't being taught! In this time that we are living in (following the COVID-19 pandemic), it will be even more important for kids and adults alike to be financially knowledgeable and secure.

The topics of finance, investing, and saving seem to scare and intimidate many people. I mean, what kind of normal teenager would be thinking about that nonsense? Even many adults brush off any notion of engaging in their financial wellbeing and saving a bit of money to help them in the future. This is the problem! Canadians are in record amounts of debt. A 2014 survey published by the CBC showed that 34% of Canadians have a well-thought-out and ingenious retirement plan; they plan to win the lottery![1] Can you believe that? The odds of winning the lottery are one in millions, and to count on that to be able to retire is absurd. Another survey reported by Bloomberg stated that 47% of Canadians said that they don't expect to cover next year's living expenses without taking on more debt.[2] All of this is a very large problem. The good news is that with this book you will learn to avoid the financial issues many Canadians are facing today. The earlier you start practising these habits, the more successful and well off you will be in the future. If I were you, I would start reading!

Chapter One

EARNING AND SPENDING

LESSON 1
Start Early

Money is a part of everyone's life. Most people love the idea of having money—who wouldn't want to be engulfed in riches? Sadly, money is a problem for most Canadians. Many adults worry about bills, paycheques, and all that nonsense. For a lot of people, there would be fewer headaches if they had learned to manage spending and saving when they were younger. If only they had read an awesome book like this one, they might have been spared a lot of trouble!

When you are young, believe it or not, you are setting yourself on a path that will shape your later life. The skills and habits that you acquire now can carry on as you grow older. If you are dedicated and have good habits, financially and in your day-to-day life while you are young, odds are you will have those same attributes as you grow up. So, the habits and skills that you acquire while you are young do matter! It's the same with money. To be well off financially and smart with your money it isn't necessary to be a high achiever of any sort. Incredibly, anyone can do it. All it takes is the practice of good habits and smart decisions. Just by reading this book you are already taking a step down the path of success for your future. To be successful in the future, you need to start practising these habits early. And what better time to start than now!

The world's highest achievers—from celebrities to athletes, to politicians, to business leaders—were often motivated from a young age; it didn't just happen for them overnight. They were also disciplined and willing to play the long game, meaning they would sometimes delay short-term gratification for bigger rewards in the future. If you want to become successful when you are older, you need to start practising for that success while you are young. Success can be anything that you want it to be. Many people think of success as being linked only with wealth; however, it can relate to everything. Success can be getting a job that you love and doing it very well. Success can be finding happiness and being true to yourself and the world. Success can be making it to the Olympics. Whatever you wish to achieve someday in the future, the best time to start on the road to getting there is now.

You can have many definitions of success. This book will help you to attain the type of success that many people wish to have when they are older: financial freedom and independence. As with all objectives and goals, the best time to start practising for your future success is now. This book will help you learn to manage your money, make smart decisions, and start growing it all from a young age. Think of this book as a first step on your personal road to future success.

From a personal point of view, success in my eyes is many things. With my running, swimming, and other sports, I want to be at the maximum level for performance and competition that my body and mind can handle. In sports, I consider improvement as well as winning to be part of success. From an academic standpoint, success can be getting good marks and learning new things. For example, if you are successful and get good grades while you are young, those good marks will open many doors later in your life, carrying that success forward. Most teens, including me, would want as many options for their future as possible. Aside from athletic and academic achievements, success for me can be applied to other areas of life. Having good friends with whom you can have fun and be yourself around. That is success, it might not be a medal or a mark, but it's definitely an achievement. Success can be found in every aspect of your life, you just have to realize what it is, and if you want it, how to achieve it. And again, the best time to start is now. Don't wait, start as early as possible.

How to Get Your Own Money

To have money you must start out either by working for it or by being privileged enough to have really generous relatives. If you are like most teens who can't rely solely on holiday and birthday money, you will need some other sources of income. The good news is there are lots of options. Mowing lawns, doing odd jobs, babysitting, shovelling driveways, getting a part-time job, and tutoring are just a few examples.

I don't tutor or have a part-time job. I earn money from mowing lawns, doing odd jobs, babysitting, and shovelling driveways. In the winter I'll go around on a school snow day and knock on the doors of people who haven't yet shovelled their driveways. About half the time they will hire me to shovel theirs for them. A tactic that's a bit risky but usually pays off is to let the client decide what to pay you. The obvious risk is that they can choose to pay you whatever they want, but for the most part I have found that they end up paying more than what is reasonable. I guess it's the mentality that they would rather be generous and pay too much than too little. On a few occasions I've made as much as $60 for one driveway! The next part of the process is to approach the well-paying clients to see if they would like me to regularly shovel their driveways. When you get a few who say yes, all of a sudden you have a steady flow of money coming in each time it snows.

I have a similar strategy for yard work. I'll first go around early in the spring and find the really messy yards that haven't yet had their spring cleanups. I'll offer the owners their choice in the amount to pay me. However, you risk getting burned if you work on someone's spring cleanup for hours and then they pay you a fraction of what is reasonable. I'll often tell my customers that I am usually paid between $15 and $20 an hour. Once I've finished they'll have seen that I work hard and do a good job, and in my experience they usually end up paying me around $22 an hour. Not bad for a kid, considering minimum wage is around $15 an hour! Once the clients are satisfied with my work, I'll ask them if anyone mows their lawn. Odds are nobody does, because if they had someone who takes care of their lawn it wouldn't have been messy in the first place. In my experience more than half the people I approach will say they don't have anyone who mows their lawn and they will hire me for the job. What I'm doing here is "business development." You first offer the prospective client a small job, and once they've seen that you did a good job they'll want to hire you for more.

A few teens have taken their ways of making money a bit further by becoming entrepreneurs. A few have even become rich and successful through their creative ideas. Here are some real-life examples of teens who really took their ideas to another level.

Examples of kid entrepreneurs

Some teenagers and kids from across the world have taken their ideas and earnings to another level. In this next section we will look into some real-life examples of kids who've created a successful business (or in some cases businesses) while they were young.

Mikaila Ulmer

It all started with two bee stings. After being stung twice in a week, Mikaila at four-and-a-half years old developed a fear of bees. Around the same time, her great-grandma Helen gave her a honey-lemonade recipe. This made Mikaila do some research and she realized how important bees are to the ecosystem and that they are endangered. Determined to do something about it, Mikaila created a product to help the cause. At the age of four she started Me & the Bees Lemonade, a flaxseed- and mint-infused lemonade sweetened with honey from local bees. For each bottle sold, Mikaila donated a percentage to charities working to save and help bees.

After originally selling her product at the local pizza place, Mikaila moved on to start showcasing and selling her product at the local Whole Foods store. After an appearance on *Shark Tank* at just ten years old, she landed an investment of $60,000 to help grow her company. Later the next year she landed an $11 million deal with Whole Foods. The rest is history. Today Mikaila sells her product in over 1,500 stores, including a new line of lip balms made with beeswax.

Evan Sharma

After visiting the Louvre at the age of ten, Evan Sharma (a fellow Kingston homeboy of mine) was immediately inspired. He was captivated by the art and in awe of the impact that a painting could have on him, often sitting in front of a single piece for hours at a time. Returning from his trip, Evan began painting on cardboard and any flat surface he could find. As a young child, after investing a small amount of money in supplies and precariously balancing on a ladder to apply paint to his large canvases, Evan began to attract some significant attention online. He applied to the Artist Project, a world-renowned Toronto art fair, and was accepted at the record-breaking age of 12!

With inspiration from the likes of Matisse and Andy Warhol, Evan's unique, vibrantly coloured acrylic pieces have been compared to the works of Basquiat, Picasso, and Matisse. At only 18 years of age, Evan now sells his paintings to private collectors all across the world, auctioning off his work for often tens of thousands of dollars. He has amassed a large social-media following; started his own clothing and sneaker fashion line, RBLB; and has even created his own non-profit, CovART Challenge, having artists donate pieces to raise money for meals for students in Kenya. Evan has already raised enough funds through his non-profit to donate over 200,000 meals, and counting.

Benjamin "Kickz" Kapelushnik

At the age of thirteen, Benjamin Kickz was just getting into the sneaker game. After getting a pair of LeBron Galaxies from his mom, he immediately became interested in the sneaker world. In fifth, sixth, and seventh grades when his parents didn't want to fund his sneaker passion anymore, he would sell candy, wash cars, walk dogs—whatever he could find to make money. Benjamin then realized that if he could pay people to stand in line to buy five to ten pairs of the hyped shoes once they came out at retail, he could then resell them, get his sneakers for free, and make a profit. Benjamin "Kickz" then found a connection to an owner of a sneaker store with Nike and Adidas contacts. When a sneaker would be released, he would pre-order pairs for just over the retail price. Benjamin says he normally looks to make a 35% to 40% profit on the sneakers he resells. Sometimes he will stockpile a certain shoe in hopes of the price rising in the future. He later met DJ Khaled through a connection. DJ Khaled needed some sneakers and soon became a regular customer and supporter of the business, introducing Benjamin to many other celebrities. Now he has sold to and supplied celebrities such as Drake, P. Diddy, DJ Khaled, French Montana, G-Eazy, Lil Yachty, Quavo, and Post Malone, to name just a few. He has over one million followers on Instagram, does millions in sales each year through an online store, and hopes to open a physical store soon in Miami, his hometown.

Caroline and Isabel Bercaw

In middle school around the ages of ten and eleven, for sisters Caroline and Isabel Bercaw, baths were a regular occurrence due to their sore muscles from their many sporting activities. To make baths less dull, they used bath bombs—small powdery balls, which, once dropped in a bathtub, erupt in fragrances and colours. They quickly realized that the store-bought ones that they were using just weren't that exciting, and they made quite a large mess. That same year (2012), they started making their own in their kitchen. By mixing baking soda, fragrance oils, and citric acid together they made a product that was up to their standards. They decided to name their company Da Bomb Bath Fizzers.

Today their company has over 200 employees, and supplies stores such as Costco, CVS, and Target with their products. In 2018, their first year, they hit $20 million in sales and they have done so every year since. In 2020 Caroline was a senior in high school, and Isabel was in her first year at the

University of St. Thomas. Their mom is now their CEO and their dad is the Chief Operating Officer. In 2015 they were selling 20,000 bath bombs a month out of their basement.

Late in 2015 their dad drove them and their product in a rented U-Haul to a Gift & Home Furnishings Market in Atlanta (both sisters were still too young to drive themselves). The market was a success and they left with 80 retailers of their product having come with only 40. The biggest was Target, with which they had landed an agreement for the retailer to sell the sisters' bath bombs in the over 1,800 stores nationwide in January 2016. The sisters now have a full office as well as a warehouse to their name.

As you can see through these examples, the sky's the limit. No matter your age you can do whatever you want to; don't think you have to wait to be "old enough." We went through only four examples but there are many, many more. If you have an idea that you think is good, don't let norms or "age restrictions" affect you. If you have a dream, go do it. And do it now. I mean, I'm in ninth grade and at the moment I'm writing a book. At first I just had the idea, but after a few months of thinking about it I realized it could actually work, and here I am a few months later writing my manuscript on my computer. Why wait to be successful and live the "dream" later in life? Why not give it a try now?

In addition to a part-time job to earn money, kids can accumulate money through an allowance or gifts from family. A study in the *New York Times* reported that the average kid has a $30 weekly allowance.[1] That's a lot of money, around $1,560 a year. I know for sure my parents have never given me that much. In fact, I have never even had an allowance. (Note: When my dad reviewed this, he thought it important to point out that although I do not get an allowance, my parents pay for my sports, clothes, and running shoes.)

As we will discuss later, financial wellbeing is determined by what you earn, how you spend, and what you save. If the average kid were to put away 10% of that $1,560 a year over six years they would have saved $936! That's only $3 of the $30 per week—they probably wouldn't even miss it. Alarmingly, most teens aren't saving anything. This means they won't have any savings when they become adults and, more importantly, they would not have developed good habits for the future.

LESSON 3
Spending Habits

Saving! It's the word that scares most people off. How am I supposed to save when I need to pay these bills, I want this, and need that? In fact, if you take a step back and look at it from a different perspective you will notice that it's not that scary at all. Spending! Much more fun and not nearly as dreadful or boring as saving. However, by controlling your spending, you can end up saving a lot of money.

The first thing to think about is what you are spending money on. Is it food? Sneakers? Video games? Clothes? Most of my money that I'm not saving and investing goes towards sports gear and clothes. When I want a new basketball, for instance, I'll go and ask my parents if they'll get me one. If they decide my current ball is still "good enough," I'll have to think about how much a new basketball is worth to me. If it is worth the $45 or so to me that it costs, then I'll think about what else I've spent money on in the past while. If I haven't done an extravagant amount of spending recently, then I will probably determine that it's worth the money.

Whatever it may be, you need to think about how much you're spending and how much it's worth to you. This is called a "cost-value analysis." You need to determine how much worth, joy, and value your spending brings you. If it is something necessary (e.g., food, clothing, transportation) or brings lots of joy to you, then this is probably something worth spending on. But on the other hand, if it doesn't meet those criteria, perhaps you should reconsider your purchase.

This raises the concept of needs vs. wants. You need food, so obviously that's something you would spend money on. However, it can get a little tricky because if you're still living with your parents, they are likely to supply you with enough food. This means that going out to dinner with your friends is a want. You must have clothes and shoes, but you don't need $400 shoes and super-expensive clothing. Again, you may want it, but you don't need it. You don't need to stop spending on all your wants. That would be no fun. You just need to determine where and what you should cut back on. If you cut back on the things that you realize don't mean much to you, you are saving money in an efficient, easy way.

Example

Matt and Dave are brothers. They each work in the plumbing industry and earn $55,000 a year. After paying taxes and essential bills such as food, clothing, and transportation, they have $5,500 leftover. Matt and Dave are both huge Raptors fans and spend $800 each year on game tickets and dates with their wives. This is a want, but something that is meaningful to them. They can either save or spend their remaining $4,700.

Matt and Dave both really enjoy coffee. Matt enjoys Starbucks and goes daily to get his $6 latte. Dave is a bit more sensical and makes his own at home. It costs Dave $8 for a pound of coffee, which works out to around 18 cents per cup. Over the course of a year, Matt will end up spending $2,190 on his lattes, and Dave will spend $66 on his homebrew. Both brothers put their remaining savings into investing. Matt puts his $2,510 in each year and Dave contributes the

$4,634 that he's got leftover. Both accounts grow by 7% each year. Dave and Matt live fulfilling lives, and other than coffee they have the same income and expenses. Now let's look into the future and see how their investments have grown. Twenty years later Matt's account will have $112,611 and Dave's will have $207,905. Already a huge gap. After fifty years, Matt's account will have $1,094,324 and Dave's will have $2,020,358! Please note, for simplicity, this example does not factor in tax, which would reduce the totals. (Taxes will be addressed later.)

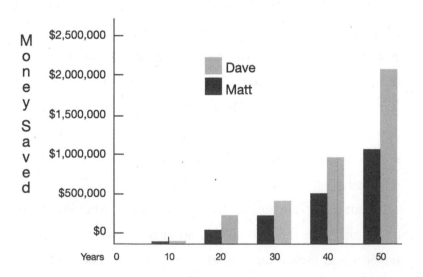

The story of these two brothers shows how cutting back on a seemingly small thing can have a huge impact on your saving! Dave realized that he didn't need a Starbucks coffee every morning and that brewing his own would do just fine.

His brother Matt liked the convenience and luxury of buying a Starbucks coffee and was willing to pay the $6 a day for it. Fifty years into the future Dave ends up with twice the money in his savings account as his poor brother Matt. They are both entering retirement and that extra million dollars makes Dave's life much more comfortable. The key lesson from this story is that by controlling your spending you are saving, and cutting back on small things can have huge benefits in the future.

When you're a teenager, material things can mean a lot. Many of us want the newest phone, the nicest sneakers, and the nicest clothes. For some people it's a status symbol, for others they just like nice things. Whatever it is, there is nothing wrong with it, but you should be smart about your purchases. You can have the newest phone for a thousand dollars, or you can buy the one that's a generation old off your friend for $30. I guess you have to be lucky enough to have a friend who would give you that kind of deal, but the idea is that if you're smart about spending decisions you can save a lot of money.

For me, my weakness is shoes, sweatpants, and hoodies. I like nice shoes and, unfortunately for my bank account, I love the fit and look of those expensive Nike sweats. If I want a nice pair of pants, Nike Tech Fleece ones for example (in my opinion the comfiest sweatpants on the market), I'll have to determine whether it's worth the price or not. Sadly, as nice as they are, Tech Fleece pants are around $120. That's a lot of money, especially for pants. And it happens to be unaffordable for most teenagers (including me). Say I really want these pants, but I'm not willing to part with the $120 that they cost. What I'll do is either wait until they go on sale, or wait until my birthday when I can hope to convince my parents to buy them. Whenever I'm buying expensive clothing or shoes I always purchase when on sale. I haven't got around to doing the math yet, but I'm sure I've saved hundreds of dollars by doing so. Another trick I've used is that if my parents are willing to buy me a "regular" pair of shoes that cost $100, but I want ones that cost $190, we purchase the shoes jointly and I contribute the extra $90. The lesson is, be smart and creative about how and when you purchase things, and the worth they are to you financially (how much money you're willing to part with in order to have them).

Vaping is a common problem today for teenagers that has implications for finances and health. It is everywhere. If you are a teenager, odds are you have encountered it in some way or another. Maybe your friends are doing it, maybe even you are. You have probably been lectured countless times by parents, teachers, and doctors on its health risks. The facts and evidence are there now, so there is no arguing that vaping is not only very bad for you, it's expensive! A recent study that looked at people aged 16 to 24 in Canada found that the average vape user spends around $17 per week on vaping.[2] Now, $17 a week might not sound like a lot, but if added up that is $884 a year. Over the course of five years that ends up being $4,420! Four thousand dollars is a lot of money, especially for someone in high school and if you were to invest that money smartly, it could end up being a lot more. Stay away from vaping because you'll be a lot richer, smarter, and healthier without it.

LESSON 4
Beware of Targeted Advertising

Targeted advertising. It's everywhere. Pop-up ads, Instagram, Snapchat, TicTok. No matter who you are, odds are you have encountered this malicious advertising software. When you are shopping online, or even just browsing the internet, big companies like Google keep track of your searches and your interests. Other companies pay for that data and then use it to advertise to you. Have you ever been looking at an item on the internet and then the next day ads are popping up on every page trying to sell it to you? It can be very tempting. It also happens to work a lot of the time. That's why companies pay millions of dollars for that data. Believe it or not, according to *Forbes*, we teenagers contribute $44 billion to the global economy each year.[3] That is a lot of money that those companies are looking to target. If you want to be responsible with your money, you will have to be aware of targeted advertising and think carefully about your purchases.

Some major companies have been accused of using algorithms to prey upon teens' emotional states and sending targeted advertising to people when they are feeling depressed or anxious. They can tell how you are feeling based on the search terms you use. These companies leverage the fact that when people are feeling down they sometimes purchase things in the hope of boosting their self-esteem.

It is so important to be aware of how sophisticated this type of advertising can be, and to try to be aware of our emotional states so that we don't unconsciously try to make ourselves feel better by making purchases. These companies know that you will get a dopamine hit from making a purchase that may temporarily make you feel a little better, but certainly won't solve your problems (dopamine is a brain chemical responsible for the feeling of pleasure). We all feel down at times, and trust me, these purchases won't make you feel better in the long run and could lead to a long-term problem with shopping addiction and debt.

LESSON 5
Financial Freedom

Money doesn't equal happiness. Although it can help with things that do. If from a young age you are smart with your money and later in life you become financially successful, you don't have to work as much and can retire earlier. A Harvard study found that adults with more free time are much happier, less depressed, exercise more, are more productive, and are less likely to get divorced.[4] All that sounds pretty nice to me. You have to realize that it's not buying things that make most people happy, but it's the freedom of being financially stable. People who live within their means are also much happier. A study done by researchers at the University of Arizona found that students who are smart with their money, save, and live within their means report better overall wellbeing and lower psychological distress.[5] Most people get pulled into the idea that consumerism will bring them satisfaction and joy. In fact, in the long run it's the opposite. Earn and save enough so you don't have to stress about bills, and happiness will follow.

LESSON 6
Beware of Credit Cards

A comment about credit cards. These very convenient (yet devious) cards end up being a part of almost everyone's life. Whether you have one now or not, you will probably acquire one when you leave your parents' house and venture off into the world. Many people find them appealing because with just a tap of a card you can purchase something that you don't even have to be able to afford when you purchase it.

Also, you can collect and accumulate points for things such as vacations, airplane tickets, and other gifts.

Sadly, as easy and appealing as credit cards may be, they can create a lot of problems for people. Essentially, a credit card is just another form of borrowing money. You use the "credit" (money borrowed from the company) to make your purchases. Each month you are required to make the minimum payments on your card balance (the amount of money owed). The problem is that many people fall for the idea that they have to pay only the minimum payments and no more. Please, I beg you, if you're reading this, never, ever pay only the minimum payments on your credit cards. Credit cards are one of the main causes of financial crises among families in North America. Credit cards have very high interest rates, where most charge 18% or more on any unpaid balance. With such high rates, credit cards are definitely not to be used for large long-term purchases. Basically, credit cards aren't to be used to buy things that you can't afford, and if you don't pay off your entire bill each month, you might as well start looking for different kinds of bankruptcy claims. Studies have shown that when you pay for something with actual cash, your brain releases the same chemicals that are released with pain. With cash you miss the money you're spending and must determine whether whatever you're buying is worth it or not. These same studies have shown that when you use a credit card, those chemicals aren't released. With a tap of a card you don't miss the money nearly as much as when you use cash. This is very dangerous to your spending habits—so much so that we will go into this in more detail in the next chapter.

Whenever I go to purchase anything, whether it be sports equipment or food, I always pay in cash. I don't use a debit or credit card. A lot of my money is invested in the stock market (more on this later), leaving very little cash in my bank account. Most jobs that I work will either pay in cash or send an e-transfer directly to my account, which I immediately invest. Either way, the only way for me to spend money is through physical cash, which I found to have made me think more about purchases and the value they have to me. When I'm older, odds are I will have to start using a debit or credit card, but for now, while I'm young, there is no need for me to use either. I encourage anyone who is still living with their parents (and even when they leave) to stay away from credit cards, unless you can always pay the bill off in full each month and you're using them just to accumulate points towards something like air miles. The only good reason to start using a credit card at a young age is to develop a good credit score (Lesson 34), but it must be done responsibly, otherwise it will have the opposite effect.

You Are Thirteen Times More Likely to Be Killed by a Hippo than Win the Lottery

"Big winnings! Lots of fun! Huge cash prizes!" To the uneducated ear this is what the promise of having a lottery ticket sounds like. Unfortunately, as enticing as they may seem, these money-burning, cash-guzzling tickets cost some people thousands of dollars over a lifetime.

Many Canadians spend hundreds of dollars a year on lottery tickets. In 2020, Ontario accounted for an estimated $4.11 billion in lottery ticket sales.[6] If you do the math, that's around $280 per person. Ninety-nine percent of the time that $280 is spent on little worthless slips of brightly coloured paper that you throw in the trash.

For every $5 ticket purchased, the odds of winning the OLG Lotto Max in Canada is one in 33,294,800. Let that number sink in, one in 33 million. To put this into perspective, here are a few things that are far more likely to happen to you than winning the lottery: being struck by lightning (about one in a million), being elected prime minister of Canada once in your lifetime (about one in 3.7 million), dying from a hippopotamus attack (one in 2.5 million), and many more. In other words, you are thirty-three times more likely to be struck by lightning, thirteen times more likely to be killed by a hippo, and nine times more likely to be elected prime minister than win the lottery.

OK. You may be thinking, "Noah, the lottery isn't all bad; there are still smaller cash prizes that you are much more likely to win and you still make a profit." Hmmm, good point, maybe the lottery is a way to earn money. Nope. Let's look at the smaller cash prizes. The smallest cash prize with Lotto Max is $20, the odds of winning that prize are one in eighty-three. Now tell me how you are not throwing away all your money. In theory, you would need to buy eighty-three $5 tickets to win $20. Now I'm no mathematician, but I think you would be losing money. Five dollars multiplied by eighty-three turns out to be $415. You can go and rub your lucky charms and use your lucky numbers all you want, but to win $20 you would lose $415.

Chapter Two

SAVING

Saving to Help Yourself Reach Your Goals

Now that you have learned about earning and spending, you might want to do something productive with the money you have. Yep, you guessed it, it's that time when we're going to cover the boring topic of saving. What you'll find is that it's not boring at all. In fact, most people who follow the rules and develop the habits that we're about to discuss find that they don't even miss the money that they're putting away. Saving is something you do to help yourself. If you start saving from a young age, you'll be supporting yourself towards future possessions you might like to have and goals you might want to achieve. Maybe you want to have a cottage, maybe you want to go on yearly vacations, or maybe you just want the mental relief of not worrying about money. These are long-term savings goals. As a teenager, you can also have short-term goals, such as buying a used car or saving money for a new snowboard. Whatever your goals and objectives may be, saving will make them possible. All you're really doing is helping yourself in the future. Trust me, you'll be thanking your teenage self for having read this book and put away a bit of money when you're in your forties and sipping a Mai Tai while looking off into the sunset on a beach at a five-star resort in Hawaii.

LESSON 9
Paying Yourself First

The best way to achieve your financial goals is to pay yourself first. What in the world does that mean? Paying yourself first is the practice of putting away money as you earn it *before* you spend it. For example, imagine you work at a part-time job for eight hours on the weekend. For those eight hours you make $120 per week (minimum wage being around $15). With paying yourself first you would put away a specific percentage of the $120. Let's say you've decided on 30% because you're a kid and you can afford to save a lot. Therefore, you would put away $36 dollars a week into a savings account of some sort. You would still have $84 dollars to spend on whatever you please. If you were to do this every week for the whole year you would end up saving $1,872 at the end of those twelve months. That's a lot of money saved, and you probably wouldn't even miss that $36 a week. Later we'll talk about how that money you saved can grow over time (hint: compound interest and investment growth!).

Essentially, all you are doing is putting money away to help your future self. Before you go and pay for the things you want, you pay yourself by saving some money. Psychologically it's a lot easier to think to yourself that this is something you have to do, so if you really want to have some extra money to buy something, you'll have to find it elsewhere. Maybe taking on some extra work for a bit more cash. On the other hand, if you were to put away money only after you finished purchasing everything you wanted, you could get carried away and have nothing left to save.

Many financial experts and institutions have referenced this method as the best and most effective way to save. When you wait until you've spent all your money, paying everyone else and then trying to save the measly amount you have left, you will find it much harder to save anything at all. By putting a predetermined amount of your earnings away you will end up saving more. What you might find surprising is that most people who practise this habit hardly miss the money once it's stashed away in a savings account. Some adults have set up investment programs that automatically take a portion of their monthly paycheque and put the funds into a savings plan. If you start practising this habit at a young age and continue into adulthood, you will be in a very good position financially.

Whenever I want to buy something worth a substantial amount of money, such as clothes, shoes, a new basketball, or headphones, I'll first check how much cash I have (money not invested). Next, I'll think about the spending I've done recently. Whether it was a lot or a little will determine if I buy the article now or wait a bit until I've earned more money.

I have a confession: Personally, I don't actually follow the pay-yourself-first method in a traditional way. This doesn't mean I think it's not important, it is for sure. The reason I don't is because of two things. One, I don't have a steady job with regular paycheques, meaning it's harder to plan to put away a specific amount of money, and two, I invest almost all my money and barely spend any in the first place! I am very fortunate to have parents who can pay for all of my basic needs, so I am able to save money. Also, I love seeing my money grow so I prefer to invest most of it rather than spend it. With the unpredictable nature of my income and my minimal spending habits, the pay-yourself-first approach just isn't necessary for me. I don't have to be rigid and structured to make smart decisions regarding my money; I trust myself fully to make good decisions. When I consider spending money, I always think about how much the item or experience is worth to me (remember the "cost-value analysis" from Lesson 3) to seek best price options. I try not to overvalue material things, I always look for better price options, and my end goal is to be financially successful and set myself up for a good future, so I am willing to limit my spending. If you're like me, then paying yourself first isn't completely necessary. On the other hand, if you have a job with regular paycheques, then paying yourself first is definitely something you should consider (especially if you tend to be a spender). When I get a job with regular paycheques, I will certainly be doing so as well. It's completely fine too if you're the type of person who needs a schedule and structure to save money, even if you don't have a regular job.

Like me, you could be someone who doesn't make a steady scheduled amount of money, you might earn a bit here and there doing jobs; you might get some from birthdays and other events. If you are someone like this, it might be hard to create a plan that you can follow in the future, but whenever you make some cash, always put away a certain amount of it before you spend the rest.

LESSON 10
Budgeting

There will come times in your life when you want to spend a lot on a specific item. In order to make a major purchase (such as a new bike or phone), you may have to save in advance for it. For these major purchases you will need to practise budgeting.

Aww man, budgeting, it's just another boring thing that adults do. As a matter of fact, budgeting is a very necessary and useful tool that will help you make decisions regarding your money that can impact the course of your life. With the ability to see where your money is coming from and going to (earning and spending), you will be able to decide what major purchases you can make and when. As we discussed earlier, by controlling spending you will have money for smaller purchases such as for shoes and clothes. In this section we will discuss how budgeting can help teenagers when it comes to larger purchases.

Let's say you want a new phone. The latest iPhone models are out and they're all much sleeker than the piece of garbage you have now. You feel that you've had your present phone for a long time and that you really deserve and need a new one. Sadly, your parents don't think the same way as you do and believe that *you* should pay for it if you want it. The new phone isn't cheap, in fact, it's around $1,000! First you need to really think about whether it is worth it to you to part with your money. Does your old phone still work? Are you falling victim to targeted advertising? Remember that material things will not provide long-term happiness, and on the flip side, being in debt causes a huge amount of stress. Think about how much that $1,000 would grow over time if you were to invest it at a young age. My point is, *really* consider whether these large purchases are worth it to you before making them.

For the sake of learning about budgeting, let's assume that you want this phone and you're willing to pay for it.

Let's say that you have $2,000 saved in an account right now. That money is invested and growing, so you really don't want to touch it. In this fictional life you're making $40 a week babysitting for a neighbouring family. You spend four hours each Friday night watching the kids while their parents go out for dinner. For this they're paying you $10 an hour. Out of that $40 you make each week, you're putting away $20 (50%). You're not going to touch that money because you're following the pay-yourself-first rule. You plan it out, and if you want to put the other $20 you have leftover each week towards your phone, it will take fifty weeks before you can purchase it. You probably don't want to wait fifty weeks, so you'll maybe want to start working some extra hours of babysitting. Say you take on an extra two hours of work and start bringing in $60 a week. You stay with your save-50% rule and now put $30 a week towards your phone. In just about thirty-three weeks you'll be able to purchase your new phone.

Finally you can buy that new phone, you're excited but you also feel proud that you followed through with the plan and turned your goal into a reality. In addition to your new phone you have $3,000 in the bank, an extra thousand dollars that wasn't there when you started saving towards that new phone. Many people would foolishly dig into their savings to buy that new phone, but you waited, budgeted, and took on a few more hours of work to pay off the phone. Believe it or not, what you just did is budgeting. You made a plan, with an end goal, then you saved and followed the plan to successfully meet your goal. And yes, budgeting can really be that easy. And on top of this, you might even enjoy your new phone more since you will know that it was within your financial means to pay for it.

On the other hand, if you had decided to dig into your savings and pay off the phone from your pool of two grand, you would be in a much different financial situation. If you continued to put away $20 from the $40 that you're making a week, by the end of the thirty-three weeks you would have around $1,660 in your bank account. That's a very different number from $3,000. With a bit of waiting, planning, and saving you can make your financial goals come true in a much more efficient and cost-effective way.

LESSON 11
Smartphones—Not Always the Smartest Purchases

Phones can cost a lot of money these days. Unfortunately, so do the plans that come with them. To reduce the amount of money pouring from your bank account to phone companies, stay away from payment plans. When purchasing a new phone, many people become suckered into the idea of "zero-dollar" phones. A lot of data-plan companies advertise the idea of getting a phone for free. What really happens is that these customers end up paying much more than they normally would have for both the phone and the plan.

The companies are not offering a phone for "free"; they are actually offering "financing" and in the long run charge you more for both the phone and the plan. This type of marketing allures people in to buying more expensive phones than they can afford and is very effective! If you think $0 phones sound too good to be true, you are right. These "deals" charge more for the phone over the period of the contract and commit you to higher monthly phone-plan rates than if you were to buy your phone upfront. You will also need to commit to a contract for a long period of time (usually 2 years) or pay high penalties to leave. You end up paying way more than if you had just bought the phone straight up and then got a plan to go with it. Don't fully trust me, go ahead and do the math yourself. Obviously, those companies aren't going to just give you a phone for free, they're going to make you pay for it and then some.

For my phone situation, I was very lucky to be able to purchase a used iPhone 6s from my friend's dad for $30. It's nothing fancy, a few generations old at the time I bought it, but considering that new iPhones cost upwards of $1,000, it was a very good deal. The reason I bought my own phone was that my parents didn't think I needed a phone and told me that if I wanted one I would have to buy it myself. I decided that if I were to spend my own money I would be as frugal as possible. I found a plan that worked for me, and went by my "frugal as possible" policy. Not much data, unlimited texting, and 100 minutes of calling. Honestly though, it's all I need, and for $15 a month, not a bad deal. After buying my phone and paying the plan for the year, I ended up spending $210. At first I was going to pay for my plan on my own, but my parents, seeing that I'd found such a low-cost option (and finally realizing that there was merit to being able to get in touch with me when I'm out), agreed to pay it for me. If I'd bought the newest phone for around $1,000 and then paid the $50 a month that most people do, I'd end up spending $1,600 in a year! That's $1,390 more than the cost of my current phone's expenses. The lesson is to always look for better prices and be frugal; small cutbacks can have huge impacts.

If you were to save that money and do something productive with it such as investing, over a few years you would notice major changes. In the first year alone you would have spent $1,390 more than it would have been if you'd gone with the cheaper scenario. Obviously the first year is the most expensive because you have to purchase the phone, but after that the phone plan that you choose can have huge impacts on your savings. After four years of going with the $50/month plan, plus the original purchase of the phone ($1,000), you would end up spending a grand total of $3,400! Almost $1,000 a year. Say you had researched the options and decided to go with the first one. You would end up spending only

$750 in four years' time, already a major difference in cost and would end up saving you $2,650! Over forty years at this the amount, you would have saved $26,500 (assuming you would be buying a new phone every four years, which most people do, if not more frequently). Not a bad chunk of extra money to have sitting around while you're in your fifties. Maybe that could be a new car? Or it could help you retire a bit earlier. If you were to invest that money, with the power of compound growth (will be discussed soon), it would be an even bigger difference. Think carefully about your spending decisions and always try to find the option with the best price-to-worth ratio.

LESSON 12
What's Worth Saving for—and What Isn't

Before anyone starts saving towards a goal, or purchase—they must think about what it is they're saving for. It is the same as spending. There are self-appreciating purchases and there are those that aren't. College or university versus a new pair of sneakers. One is setting you on a path for your future and can help you acquire a good job and earn money, whereas the other is just a material object that might last you a year or two. I am not saying that all our purchases have to be practical—it's OK to sometimes buy things just for fun! What I am saying is that we need to recognize which saving and spending goals will lead to long-term satisfaction and which ones are for short-term gratification.

One of the more complex ideas when thinking about your purchases is self-appreciating vs. depreciating assets. I know it sounds complicated. All this means is that some things go up in value after purchase, whereas others don't. As soon as you take a brand-new car off the lot, it's worth can go down by a tremendous amount. Most of the time in the thousands of dollars. Used cars are cheaper and do not depreciate as much as new cars. The first three cars my parents bought for our family were all used cars. The only car they bought "new" was a 2010 minivan, which they still drive over a decade later. My family certainly does not have the nicest cars in the neighborhood (due to the age of each of our two cars and how my three younger siblings trash them with their snacks and toys), but making these decisions probably allowed my parents to save money for other things, such as going on family trips.

On the other hand, when you purchase something like a house, the value can go up. In most places where real estate is being sold and new people are moving into the area, the prices of homes and properties rise. This may not happen forever, and there have been examples of the real estate market crashing in the past, such as in 2007–2008. However, for the most part people sell their homes for more than they bought them for. When purchasing, think about what the value of the item might be when you want to sell it. Another savings goal that will yield benefits in the future is your education; saving for university or college is a short-term financial sacrifice, but in the long-term it can improve your financial situation tremendously by allowing you to get a better-paying job.

To return to the phone in our example, if you decide to purchase a newer and more expensive phone, you might consider how much you could sell that phone for when you're ready to move on and buy a new one. If you can sell it for a reasonable price that will help you buy the new phone, then sure, go ahead, that might be an investment worth making. When you look at your purchases this way, you're starting to do something from which many people have made successful careers. You're buying low and selling high. When you buy something with hopes to sell it for more, you are investing money in said product. Many people do this for a living. Ever heard of a stockbroker? An investment advisor? These people make investments for a living (and some make a lot more than just for a living, mostly in the stock market). They buy stocks and then hope to sell them for more than what they bought them for. Don't worry, this will all make much more sense later.

Example: *Reselling sneakers*

A common example of teenagers investing in something is the buying and reselling of sneakers. Whether you have an interest in shoes or not, it is a very interesting approach that some teens use to earn money. Some teens these days are buying hyped-up shoes straight from the retailer before they sell out. The retail price of these shoes isn't anything special; for the most part they sell for around the same as any other shoe at retail. The thing is, they sell out fast. If you are lucky enough to get a pair, you can look to sell them for much more than what you bought them for. Some shoes will skyrocket in price after they are released. The limited quantity and the hype around them make people willing to pay the ridiculous prices for these shoes. Websites like StockX and GOAT make it easy for people to resell their sneakers to potential buyers. You can upload the shoes you bought onto these sites and then sell them for substantially more than you bought them for.

Take the Nike Air Max 90 OFF-WHITE Black for example. For those of you who don't know, Off-White is an Italian luxury fashion label founded by American designer Virgil Abloh. They sometimes will do shoe collaborations with Nike. When this particular sneaker, the Nike Air Max 90 OFF-WHITE Black came out on the Nike website, it sold at retail for $220 CDN—the normal price for a Nike sneaker. Those lucky enough to have purchased it at that price can now sell it, at the time of this writing, for $920 because, like stock prices, the value of certain shoes can rise and fall for numerous reasons. In this example, it was an easy $700 profit! However, be aware that there is risk in every investment. If you do decide to try to buy and resell products such as shoes, do your research and calculate how risky it may be and whether you will make your money back.

LESSON 13
Small Savings, Big Impacts

Cumulative small savings can have very large impacts on your financial situation. What that means is that if you can cut back and save a little on lots of small items, you can end up saving a lot overall. Say you spend $5 on two packs of your favourite gum from the corner store every week. Over a year you would end up spending $260 just on gum! If you were to start going to a cheaper option, a dollar store for example, where gum packs are only $1(!), you could end up saving a lot of money.

If you were to go to the dollar store instead of your local corner store and spend $2 a week on gum, you would end up spending only $104 a year. That's a lot less than $260! You would cut back and save $156 from that one small fiscally smart move that you made. An extra $156 can be quite noticeable for someone in high school. That money could go towards something more valuable to you than gum. You could invest that money and make a profit off it, or you could maybe even finally afford that new phone you wanted. And the best part is you're still getting your dose of gum every week, but you might be travelling just a few minutes further to get it.

Obviously this is a pretty random and specific example; however, it can be applied to almost everything. Some easy examples include making your own lunch at home instead of buying from the school cafeteria or nearby fast-food joints and being mindful of unnecessary spending at coffee shops, corner stores, and vending machines. Now let's say you were able to cut back on all your regular purchases. You've seen how much something small like gum can do, imagine what would happen if you did that for everything; the results could be extraordinary! It takes some problem solving and research, but you can do it!

When my mom was a teenager, she had great jobs working at a movie theatre and waitressing in a restaurant. She used to regularly collect $50 to $100 in tips a day on top of her salary, but she regrets that she didn't save anything, spending it all on clothes and eating out. Can you imagine how much money that would be worth now, some thirty years later, if she had invested it? The answer is a lot.

If you take the responsibility to investigate ways that you can cut back on your spending, you can have a huge impact not only on your present life but also on your future. If you were to save and invest the money that you are cutting back on, you could have a huge leg up when you go to university, or when you're looking into buying a house. It takes just the little things. Waiting to buy on sale, price searching, and determining how much something is worth to you. When you take the initiative to practise this, you will very quickly start seeing the results.

LESSON 14
Keeping Track of Your Money's Comings and Goings

Keeping track of the comings and goings of your money is pretty easy with a basic spreadsheet. In a spreadsheet you enter how much you're making in a certain period of time and look at how much you are spending and where that money is going. This can be really eye-opening for some people. You might not realize how much you're spending on some items that aren't even that important to you. Maybe you're that person who's spending $20 to $25 dollars a month on gum and you didn't even know it until you charted where your money was going. I guarantee that the teenagers who are buying coffee from Starbucks several times a week would be shocked if they saw their total spending on coffee per month! This practice can help you drastically cut back on purchases for which you might be spending more than you realize is reasonable. Using a spreadsheet to keep track of your money is a very good and efficient way to make a lot of cumulative small savings and keep track of your progress—with earnings and with savings. You can use online spreadsheets like Excel or Google Sheets, or you can use charted paper. An even easier option (and probably more convenient in most cases), is to download a budgeting app on your phone. This way you can keep track of your spending as you buy items, and you don't need to remember everything once you get home. All of these options are good; you just have to choose the one that's best for you.

LESSON 15
The Life-Changing Power of Compound Growth

One of the most powerful financial tools and concepts is—wait for it, Drrrrum roll, please—the Power of Compound Growth. This is an extremely important and essential concept that will help you grow and amass your money. The power of compound growth is the holy grail of investing, the sacred truth of finances. And the great thing is that it's not complicated or even hard to understand.

Let's think of it like this: You earn money; it could be from doing whatever you wish—building rocket ships, mowing lawns, whatever you want it to be, it doesn't matter. When you earn money from your sources of payment it grows more and accumulates more and more as you continue to earn and grow your wealth. If you were to stash all of your earnings in a safe, the only logical way for it to grow, or accumulate, would be by adding more to the safe. Now there is another way to grow that money that is going to blow your mind. If you were to put that money in a bank account, or invest it in commodities, bonds, or the stock market (don't worry, we'll touch on those later), it can grow and multiply even faster. It could be in a bank account where the bank pays you a very small percent of your money back in interest for storing it there. Or it could be the growth of stocks and commodities that you purchase, and perhaps pay you dividends (another subject for later). Whatever it may be, your money is growing over time, and with that growth an interesting math concept and principle comes into play. Your money starts to compound on itself. Because your money is growing by a percentage of itself, with more money it will grow by more. Ten percent of a thousand is more than ten percent of a hundred. As the percentage of your earnings is added to your money, the percent will be worth more each year as the total amount of your money increases. You can actually earn interest on your already-earned interest! Don't worry, in the chapters ahead we will go over the topics of investing and trading, and all this will make much more sense.

Example: *The power of compound growth*

Ethan is a smart kid. He earns money shovelling driveways in the winter, mowing lawns in the summer, and babysitting for the neighbours year round. Ethan has been saving his money for the past four years. By his fifteenth birthday he had earned and saved a total of $5,000. He recently read an outstanding book on finances by the one and only David Chilton, *The Wealthy Barber: The Common Sense Guide to Successful Financial Planning*. The book inspired him, so he decided to take his finances a step further. He used that $5,000 to buy into an "index fund" (don't worry, this will be touched on later). He made a good decision because the index fund went up 7% over the course of that year. At the end of the year his shares in the index fund were worth $5,350; he had made a solid $350 in that one year. Ethan decided to reinvest all the money he made. The index fund had an average annual growth of 7% and continued to do so for the next three years. The second year came around, and it was Ethan's seventeenth birthday, which he decided was an appropriate time to check how much his index fund was worth. He was delighted to see that it had gone up another 7% since he'd last checked, and was now worth $5,724.50. At the end of his high-school career (after three years of investing), Ethan decided it was time to cash out on his index funds. He was heading to college and needed the money for his first year of tuition. He ended up selling it for $6,125.20. Without adding any money at all, his $5,000 had gone up just over $1,000. Not bad for three years. And all of that increase came from the power of compound growth.

Now let's use some bigger numbers with higher percentages. Say you put $1 million into a bank account and invest-
ed that money by buying stocks. You do quite well and have
an annual average return of 10%. Ten percent of a million
is $100,000. After one year your *portfolio* (a word for your
group of stocks) would be worth $1,100,000, the next year
you make 10% again ($110,000; 10% of $1,100,000). At the
end of the year you have a total of $1,210,000. You keep your
money in the investment and make another 10% ($121,000)
over the course of the year. You now have $1,331,000. You
continue to do this each year. By four years you would have
$1,464,100, by five years you would have $1,610,510, by six
years you would have $1,771,561, and after seven years you
would have $1,948,717. (For simplicity, tax considerations
are not included in this example. Also, growth of an index
fund usually has two components: increase in stock values
and dividends paid. Dividends can be reinvested to buy more
stock. This and tax issues will be discussed later.)

In seven years, your money practically doubled without
adding any extra cash to the account. All that has been hap-
pening is the value goes up and then compounds and continues to do so over the course of a long period of time. If
this were to continue, after twenty years you would have a
whopping $6,727,500! Now you can see how powerful com-
pound growth can be. You started out with a million dollars
and after twenty years it grew by $5,727,500. That's almost

600% growth with earning 10% a year for twenty years. In fact, this is how the rich keep on getting richer. Some people are so wealthy that they don't even touch their savings; they live off just their investment income! Imagine that you have a billion dollars. Say your money grows on average by 3% each year, nothing special. From a billion dollars that 3% becomes $30,000,000! For the most part, billionaires hardly ever touch their savings for personal use. One of the only reasons they will dig into their savings would be to invest in something in the hope that their money will grow by even more. (Note: These examples do not include capital gains tax, which is covered in chapter five. I did not include taxes in these calculations because tax rates vary depending on where you live, and you don't need to pay tax on capital gains until you sell your investments.)

You could keep doing this as long as you want. There is a little formula with which you can determine how many years it will take to double your money at a certain percentage of interest. It's called the Rule of 72. What you do is take the average percentage that your money grows each year and divide 72 by it. With the 10% growth it would take 7.2 years for your money to double ($72 \div 10 = 7.2$) just by sitting there and accumulating. Therefore, the higher the percentage the shorter the length of time it takes for your money to double. Pretty simple math.

Therefore, it is so important to start saving and investing early! You've seen how powerful growth compounding is over time. The earlier you start the more your money will grow. Time is the most essential tool to growing your money. If you start young you will have a huge advantage and leg up in the world when you are older. The power of compound growth is essentially made up of two ingredients: cumulative growth rate plus time. You need to have your money growing at a certain rate over a certain period of time, and then repeat. The more time you have the larger the sum will be. Lost time isn't something that can be made up for; once you lose it, it's gone. Don't waste and lose the precious time that you have now, go ahead and start putting that money away into investments anywhere it will grow. With the growth over a long period of time, your money will start to increase at faster and faster rates, all thanks to the power of compound growth.

Here is a chart to show the power of compound growth over a period of time at a 7% rate of increase.

Compound Growth with 7% Increase per Year with a One-time Deposit of $2,000		
Years elapsed	Total Value of Portfolio	Total Growth Earned
Original Deposit	$2,000.00	$0.00
After One Year	$2,140.00	$140.00
After Two Years	$2,289.80	$289.80
After Three Years	$2,450.08	$450.08
After Four Years	$2,621.59	$621.59
After Five Years	$2,805.10	$805.10
After Ten Years	$3,934.30	$1,934.30
After Twenty Years	$7,739.37	$5,739.37
After Fifty Years	$58,914.05	$56,914.05

LESSON 16
The Real Rate of Return

When making investment decisions and calculating how much you hope to make from them there is something that you need to keep in mind. It is called the "real rate of return."

The real rate of return is what your earnings are after inflation. Inflation is the decreasing value of money. Each year the Canadian dollar is worth less and less. This is because of a lot of factors such as the servicing of debt and the printing of money that are complicated, and there is no need for us to get into this area.

When your parents were kids, a single dollar could purchase a lot more than it can today. For example, as I am writing this book, buying a bottle of Coca-Cola can be around $2. When my grandparents were in their teens, they could purchase a bottle of Coke for as little as a nickel. If you leave money just sitting in cash, it actually decreases in value. Four hundred dollars might have been a lot of money 150 years ago, but now it's worth a lot less. This is why it's important to invest and find ways to grow your money so that, at the very least, you avoid having your money decrease in value due to inflation.

Each year the Canadian dollar succumbs to inflation of 2% give or take. When you are calculating how much you make off an investment, you have to keep that in mind. Say you make exactly 2% more each year, you would then just be breaking even, earning and losing no money. However, say you put money into a low-earning savings account, a GIC, or a chequing account. You could potentially be losing money if your earnings are lower than yearly inflation. Therefore, when calculating your earnings you have to adjust for the real rate of return, adding inflation into the equation. For example, say you made 7% in earnings from your investment one year and the Canadian dollar was inflated by 2% that same year, you are really only ahead 5% (your real rate of return).

Another factor you should consider is how much you're paying your financial advisor (if you have one) vs. the amount that you earn. It's the same concept. Say you pay 3% of all your money each year to your financial advisor or stockbroker. To earn anything at all, you would have to make over 5% a year due to 2% inflation and 3% of your money going to whomever you are paying to invest your money. This can be eye opening for some people. You may be earning a lot less than you think. Keep these two "real rate of return" factors in mind when you are dealing with your money.

Chapter Three

YOUR FUTURE

LESSON 17
Start Young

The reason people save money and invest is to help their future selves. When deciding between investing and spending your earnings you must decide between small instant gratification and the long-term larger benefits of saving. The power of compound growth and long-term investment returns will make your money worth far more in the long term. For adults who pay their own bills, feed their kids, pay for their sports, and plan family vacations, it can be much harder to save. While you are a kid, you're blessed with the freedom of fewer responsibilities. You don't have to pay the bills, you can save most of what you earn, and you can still have fun being a kid! This time also happens to be an opportunity when you can set yourself on a very promising track for your financial future. For kids who are in more challenging situations, where they are depended on to bring in money to support their families, developing good financial habits is just as important, if not more so. When you are young, you have the opportunity to positively impact your future; all you have to do is act on it.

LESSON 18
Future Goals

Many teenagers have dreams or goals for their future. When you're young you can have all kinds of dreams about what you want to do when you're older. Some kids want to become prime minister or rule the world (as does my sister Lilah); others want to play professional sports (like my brother Everitt) or become a famous musician (like my sister Adele). Whatever it is, when you are young you set yourself on a path for your future. If you want to be an astronaut, a teacher, a lawyer, or a doctor, you have to work hard in school and do your best. If you want to become a professional athlete, you have to practise to achieve your maximum potential in the sport. Whatever it is you want to do, you need to start practising for that goal as soon as the desire pops into your mind.

Goals don't always have to be about your career. They can be simpler than that. Being fit and healthy is a goal, having a summer cottage is a goal, exploring the world is a goal, learning a new language is also a goal. A goal can be whatever you want it to be. The dictionary defines a goal as the object of a person's ambition or effort, an aim or desired result. There you have it. A goal is just the expression of something that you want to achieve.

A goal for some people might be to be financially comfortable or wealthy when they're older. Who doesn't want to be rich? Or at least financially comfortable? Being financially comfortable can mean taking vacations all over the world. It can mean working fewer hours or retiring earlier and spending more time with your family. For many young people the answer would be, yes, one of my goals is to do well financially when I'm older. Even if your goals are focused elsewhere, being financially stable will help you achieve those other goals. And as we discussed earlier, the best time to start to reach those goals is now, while you are young.

Although I play many sports competitively, running is my main focus. Both my parents still run and were competitive runners in high school and university, so I've always been exposed to the sport. In elementary school I started running cross-country and road races. I came second at my first race in grade four, and I still remember it. Being the regional cross-country meet, there were still the city finals left. I pushed through the championship race and managed to win by over 300 metres, and I've been hooked ever since. I have continued with running because I love the competition and rawness of the sport. For the foreseeable future, running is something that I want to continue into university and further into the future. However, running isn't the only goal that I have in mind. I also want to have a career that is interesting and meaningful and become financially stable in the future. Another personal goal is to publish a successful book that can help kids all over the world. And on that note, I'd like to thank you, my readers, for helping with that particular goal!

LESSON 19
Financial Side of Post-secondary Education

One goal that many teens strive for is to attend college or university. Although there are many obvious upsides to attending college and university, it is a costly phase of life. University tuition in Canada can cost from $4,000 to $20,000 a year, and that doesn't even include books! If you are moving into an apartment or residence you will have to pay for rent, food, and utilities. On top of this, you are in school for eight months of the year, and it is difficult to earn money while at school. All that being said, you do have four months in the summer to work. But that time isn't always enough to earn enough for tuition and living expenses. The reality is that most teens attending college or university will rely on help from their parents (if they are able) and/or to some degree take on a student debt.

Other very helpful financial aids for university are scholarships and bursaries. Many people think that scholarships are only for the geniuses with the top marks and elite athletes. However, there are scholarships and bursaries independent of marks or sports for students with many different backgrounds and interests. There are scholarships for activities such as volunteering, and various clubs and wealthy alumni often sponsor kids from their old high schools to attend university. In fact, an analysis done by the CBC found that 40% of students in Canada attending full-time post-secondary education (college or university) are granted free tuition.[1] Perhaps the cost for books and meals for those 40% of students isn't included, but this shows that it is possible to substantially reduce the total cost for a post-secondary education. Do some research on various types of scholarships and learn what they are looking for and how to apply for them.

The good news is that there are student debt packages with very low interest rates and many, including the Ontario Student Assistance Program (OSAP), do not charge interest until after graduation. The bad news is that many students take on more debt than necessary through careless spending habits, resulting in their having to carry that debt onward into their later life. Having large amounts of debt can lead to later retirements or even require young adults to work a long time after graduation before realizing some of their dreams. People with large amounts of debt may not be able to support their children financially through college or university. This leads to their children's racking up larger amounts of debt, and so forth in the vicious cycle.

If you intend to go to college or university, the best time to start planning is now. Start saving, look into investing your money, and keep learning and developing smart spending habits. Minimizing spending on education after high school is so important because it will result in being able to pay off your education debt earlier and start saving and getting on with your life. The goal during this phase of your life should be to minimize spending and debt so that you can pay it off as soon as possible once you graduate and start making money. By following the principles and lessons in this book, you will help yourself get through university, and therefore set yourself and your future family on a successful path for the future.

LESSON 20
The Best and Most Important Investment Is—Yourself!

The definition of investing is to put time or money into something in the hope of a greater return than what you put in. Yes, investing your money is important if you want to be financially successful in the future (again, we will talk about that later). But what many people don't realize is that it is just as important to invest in yourself. Investing in yourself can be whatever you think will make you a better person, such as being more capable, being happier, accomplishing purposeful things, or achieving more. For example, education is an investment in yourself. With a good education you can open the doors to many different career paths. This could lead you to getting a job that you really enjoy and that is better paying. Without spending the money to go to university or college, you would likely never have the opportunity to get the job you want. With a higher-paying job, you will make more than what you spent on education, therefore making it a good investment.

Other types of self-investment can include purchasing a gym membership or joining a mindfulness course. For example, the gym membership would help you become physically fit. Being fit can not only make you feel better, but it can also increase your productivity and mental wellbeing. Aside from the obvious benefits to your being healthy and active, it can make you more productive and in a better mood, which can lead to your making better financial decisions and operating at a higher level in your job. This can lead to better career opportunities and promotions. The money you earn from the increase in salary can pay off your investment in something like a gym membership or joining a sports team. All of this could boost your confidence and self-esteem, leading to even more success.

The same can be said for a mindfulness course. Many studies show that mindfulness and meditation can make people operate at a higher level in anything from sports to business. Not only can being mindful make you a better and happier person, it can also help you make better spending/ saving choices, thus benefitting you financially too. When buying items such as road bikes and memberships, just think about whether or not it is a self-investment and what the payout or gains are. This can help when making decisions on spending. Meditating just a few minutes a day has been proven to improve memory and concentration, boost the immune system, decrease depression and anxiety, reduce stress, and even make you kinder. There are many free online resources to develop a mindfulness and meditation practice. There are also some apps worth paying for, including Ten Percent Happier, which my mom uses. (My mom suggested I put this in—surprise, surprise!)

Many of us won't need to worry about many expenses until we leave our parents' home. At the moment, my parents pay for my food, most of my clothes, my sports, physiotherapy, the dentist, haircuts, and so on. When I leave my parents' house it will be a very different story; I will be paying for everything and making decisions on what to spend on and what not to. Since I'm really into sports, exercise, and fitness, I plan to spend money on stuff like gym memberships, healthy organic food, and the necessary gear and equipment to stay active. Maybe I'll spend a lot on something like a road bike, or a treadmill so I can run even on days in the winter when the road hasn't been cleared. These are all examples of some things that I'll likely consider important self-investments for my future.

LESSON 21
All Those Careers

One topic that isn't taught or talked about enough in school is the financial aspect of different career paths. Few people are in a position where they can do whatever they want, no matter the salary, and then be able to live the lifestyle they want. Some people would argue that you should pick a job that makes you happy, and they are correct. But there is a fine balance between the love for your job and the salary and benefits that it may provide. With a well-paying job, you will be happier and less burdened outside of work. With a low-paying fun job that you love, you will be happy at work, but when you come home to bills and money worries, that can change. Nobody wants a job that they absolutely hate, and nobody wants a job that they can't live off. The key is to find a balance between them.

Nowadays (and it's probably been like this forever), there can be a lot of pressure on kids to choose certain careers early. Most parents want to see their kids grow up and become "successful," but really, what does successful even mean? Many teenagers and adults consider success around a few things: Money, Status, Prestige. These three things determine the stereotypical level of success of career paths and jobs. Yet true success is happiness and contentment. Meaningful achievement can be a key ingredient for contentment. And yes, the financial payoff of a job is important. But more important is to do what you love.

In my experience, a lot of kids have no idea what they want to be when they are older—including me. Running is definitely something that I want to pursue; one day I hope to compete for Team Canada. But after that (because no one stays an elite runner their whole life), I have no clue what I want to go into. Like everyone, I have fields of interest, such as finance, medicine, and athletics, but at this point in my life I have no job or career plans that I'm really invested in. Just thinking from a logical point of view, this would mean I should keep as many doors open as possible. If I don't yet know what I want to do, I'd like to have as many options as possible to choose from when the time comes. I'd recommend this to everyone. Stay in school and work hard just to keep as many doors open as possible. You will thank your younger self for doing so.

Chapter Four

AN INTRODUCTION
TO INVESTING

LESSON 22
Interest Is Free Money

Interest is free money. That's what it is. The reason people invest, trade, or put their money in a high-interest savings account is to make money. To live nowadays you need money; it's just a necessary part of life. From food, shelter, water, and healthcare to all the other basic necessities for living, money is required. Whether it is money spent by the government or yourself, it doesn't happen for free. If you want to travel the world, you need money. If you want food and clothes, you need money. If you want transportation, you need money.

Money is a measurement of wealth and a tool to trade for other goods or services. In one form or another, money has been around for at least three thousand years, and before then, bartering and trading was used. And most likely some form of money will be used for at least another three thousand years. Humans have evolved to trade among and between one another, and to do this, some kind of currency was necessary. It is interesting to think that a few hundred years ago money was in the form of gold coins, then it became coins made with other metals and paper bills, and then it was exchanged electronically by the tap of a plastic card, and now we have crypto currencies!

Investing is a way to make your hard-earned money work for you—at least it better because you sure worked for it! That's the miracle of interest and cumulative growth (compound growth). By investing your money you can basically bring in free money. Yes, it does take some time, and there is risk involved, but I think most people want to have as much money as possible, and by investing your money you can grow your wealth without working extra hours at your job.

The real question is, why isn't everyone taking advantage of the ability to grow their money? I would think everyone would want to grow their wealth by as much as possible, right? The main reason teenagers like you and me aren't investing their money is that they don't know a thing about it. The average adult views investing and the stock market as some high-profile centre where complex trading happens in which only geniuses with vast amounts of money can partake. Teens on the other hand have never or rarely been taught about it. Funnily enough, recently the main source for teenagers to learn about investing is coming through Reddit chat forums.

Before I read *The Wealthy Barber* (the first personal-finance book I ever read), I didn't have any idea about what investing was, or even what it meant to buy a stock. I had a vague idea that it was a full-time career for very intelligent adults. However, the financial books I read enlightened me to the fact that anyone can invest their money and take advantage of the opportunity to grow it. After that I started saving my money and investing it with the help of a few other people. You can do the same too. I really wish this stuff was taught more in schools as it is so important and really quite simple.

LESSON 23
Financial Securities

As you go deep into the world of investing and trading, you need to understand a few basics. First, what is a stock? All a stock really is, is a small piece of a company that was sold to raise money. Imagine two kids starting a lemonade stand. Initially business is slow, but after a few months their business is doing well. The business is bringing in a lot of money, and the owners decide that it's time to expand their lemonade company. They decide that the best way to increase sales and, as a result, profits, is to buy a lemonade factory. However, they don't have enough money to buy the factory, so they decide the best way to raise money is to sell shares of their company to the public. They sell a certain percent of their company with an estimation of how much it's worth. Let's say they think their business is worth $100,000. They could then sell shares for 40% of the business (they would probably want to remain majority owners, keeping 60% for themselves, and receiving the $40,000 cash from selling 40% of the shares to help build their company). This gives them the cash to buy the new factory and expand their business. Now people can buy, sell, and trade their shares of the lemonade company.

This is a simple example of what happens with really big companies in the real world. When a company wants a new factory, or to fund a new project, they'll sell off more shares. The owner/founder has to be smart about how much of their company they'll sell off. If they sell too much while the company is starting, they won't have any assets of their own that can grow and earn them money, and they will lose control of the company's direction. On the other hand, raising money will help the company expand and grow, making their shares and percentage of the holding grow in value. Owning shares gives you the right to help make decisions for your company, whereby one share is worth one vote. When people own a large proportion of a company's shares, they will likely provide input on decisions and plans for the company. The board of a company is often made up mostly of the big shareholders.

When you buy a stock, you are making a bet on the company. If the company does well, you will make money; if the company flops, you will lose money. The simplest yet truest rule of investing is "buy low, sell high." Believe it or not, that's the formula for making money. When deciding what stocks to buy, there are endless calculations and methods to help you make your decisions. When it all comes down to it, no one on this planet knows what's going to happen to the stock market. Many experts will say they have the formulas and knowledge to find all the winner "good stocks," but in reality no one ever completely beats the stock market. Even the best of the best suffer losses—and make wrong decisions. One general rule is that if you buy shares in high-quality companies and you are able to keep your investment for the long term, you will likely make money. However, this isn't always the case, even big stable companies can suffer losses. Later we will look at what makes a stock or company a good investment. Stocks aren't the only financial security you can trade or invest in; commodities, currency, crypto, and real estate are three examples of other types of investments.

The first example, commodities, are raw materials. Some commodities you might have heard of would be products such as gold, oil, and coffee. The value and price for these items goes up and down over time due to supply and demand and popularity, similar to shares of a company. This means there is an opportunity for investors to make money. The second example, currencies, such as US dollars and Swiss francs, can also go up and down in their relative value depending on the economy of the country. Some people will have a lot of one kind of currency and potentially convert it to another when it is high in relative value. For example, if the US economy is very strong, investors from other countries might want to use their own currency to purchase US dollars. Unfortunately for the average investor, investing in commodities and currency is extremely risky and volatile. Big investment houses, banks, and hedge funds play in this game, but without sophisticated knowledge of global economic and political factors—and access to huge resources to monitor them—it is almost impossible for a novice or hobby investor to be successful in this area.

The third investment that some people make is in real estate. Real estate is highly sought after, and for the most part increases in value over time. Large real estate companies will buy property in a place that is growing in population and later sell it for a lot more. For example, a $600,000 house bought in Toronto in 2010 could easily be worth $1,200,000 in 2021. That's just one example of money that can be made. Again, there is risk in the real estate market and expenses such as property taxes associated with owning a house.

As a kid, odds are you don't even come close to having enough money to start buying real estate; however, it's something to think about when you are older. Among the examples I have just given, the stock market is probably the most sensible first place to invest money as a teenager with the advice of a professional advisor, especially when you are starting out and learning.

The stock market historically earns around 6% to 7% a year, which is much higher than you can expect to earn in a savings account in recent years (usually 0.01% to 1.5%), but some risk is involved. It's important to diversify your stocks to minimize your risk (and not invest in one or just a few companies that could tank). Remember the old saying, "Don't put all of your eggs in one basket!" It's better to spread the risk across many different companies and sectors—some will be winners, and some will be losers, but overall if your stock portfolio is diverse enough it should increase in value over time (barring any major world economical disasters).

To own a diverse portfolio of stocks, an investor needs to have several thousand dollars, which can be tough for teens starting out in investing. Don't worry! There is a solution to this problem: Investment products such as index funds and exchange traded funds (ETFs) allow you to invest in the stock market in a diverse way without needing a lot of money to start out with. These funds pool money from many investors to buy a wide variety of stocks, bonds, or securities. They are a good option if you don't have a lot of money to invest, and to minimize your risk through diversification. Index funds also typically have low management fees and outperform similar products such as mutual funds—another bonus! Talk to a financial advisor and they will discuss index funds and many other investment options with you. Just remember to consider the fees from both the investment products and the advisor, and any tax implications when you are estimating your potential return.

LESSON 24
Traders, Investors, and the Great World of Money

Before I get too far ahead of myself, let's break down investing and trading a bit more. There are two main categories of people in the stock market. There are traders and there are investors. Now you may be wondering what the difference is, aren't they both buying stocks? In fact, there is a world of difference.

First, let's start with traders, in particular the "day traders." You may have heard of them as the people who take big risks and make a lot of money. In reality, day trading is quite risky and a very time-consuming task. Day traders try to take advantage of small dips and movements in a stock's price from day to day, or even from hour to hour. They like to buy in and sell out in a relatively short period of time. A day trader's goal is to make lots of small profits over the day. When day trading you rarely look into or care about the fundamentals (the companies' values, policies, and such) of a company, and instead focus only on the numbers. Day traders rarely hold stocks for more than a few hours. And it's even rarer for them to hold onto a stock overnight—hence the name "day trader." Day trading can be risky with the potential to lose a lot of money. To be successful as a day trader you have to put in a lot of hours of work. Day traders are always watching every movement of the stocks that they trade in. For most of them it becomes a full-time job.

A less extreme example of trading is the practice of something called "swing trading." Swing traders are also traders looking to buy into stocks and sell out with a profit. The difference is that instead of following small dips and rises, they look for longer-term movements (or "swings") in their stocks, commodities, or currencies. An example of a swing trade would be to buy into a company before a new product is launched in the hope of it being successful, and then selling once the shares have gone up. Swing traders will look more into the fundamentals of a company than a day trader. Factors such as new CEOs, new products and policies, and so on, all have impacts on the investments and trades a swing trader will make. Major market corrections can also provide opportunities for profitable swing trading. For example, some people made huge profits buying good-quality stocks when the market tanked due to COVID-19 concerns in March–April 2020.

A third kind of person in the stock market is the "investor." Investors don't worry about quick trades. They look for stocks that have good potential for a steady future growth. Investors buy and hold for a longer period of time than traders would. An investor might look for stocks that historically have been climbing steadily. Another attribute of a stock that investors look for are dividends. A dividend is a distribution of a portion of a company's profits to its shareholders. Usually dividends are a small percentage of the holdings you have where the companies will pay on a scheduled basis (such as monthly, quarterly, or annually). With the growth of the stock over time, plus dividends, this can be attractive to many investors. Some experienced investors consider regular and increasing dividends to be a sign of a well-managed company that is likely to continue growing in value.

LESSON 25
Good Investments and Bad Investments

What makes a good investment? What makes a bad investment? These are two simple questions with simple answers, the only problem is that sometimes it can be challenging to tell the difference between the two.

A good investment, in its simplest form, is when you put time, effort, or money into something to see benefits and reward. In finances we most often deal with investments in companies. When you buy shares of a company, to help it raise money, you want to see positive growth. Basically, you want your money to increase in value with the company that you bought into. A good investment is when you buy stocks of a company that continues to grow in a manner that results in your making a profit when you sell it. It's even better when the company also pays you dividends along the way, while you wait for their stock price to grow. A bad investment is when you put money into a company that starts to do poorly and decreases in value, losing your money. Sounds simple enough, but how can you tell the two apart?

There is a long list of conditions that you can look for when deciding what companies to buy into. Some of the most important, and most basic include the following: Is the company a strong, stable company with a good history? Are there any factors to take into account that might boost or hurt this company's growth? And is now the right time to buy?

Let's start with the first. Looking into a company's history, and knowing about the company, is one of the most important things to look for before investing. You should never buy a stock without knowing a lot about the company you are buying into; if you know nothing, then all you are doing is gambling. Companies with good track records for the most part, but not always, continue to do well. To do so well, these companies have been doing the right things, which usually means they have management who will respond well to changing circumstances, and will continue to perform. At the same time, you want a company that has done well for a long time, and the longer the better. Yes, sometimes there can be good investment opportunities in new companies, but there is also a lot more risk as there isn't a long period of time for you to see how they have performed. In general, knowing about the company and looking into its history is a key factor when it comes to investing.

Second, are there any factors that can boost or hurt this company's growth? Before investing, you want to think about and take in all the variables that could have an impact on the success of the company. Is the field in which the company deals growing or decreasing? For example, with the huge movement by government and companies towards fighting climate change and going green impacting new policies, you might not want to buy into an industry such as oil and gas (in addition to environmental and ethical considerations). Is the company about to implement new policies or changes that might be positive or negative for future growth? Many things can change the course of a company, so you have to do your research and think about how they can impact your investing.

And third, is now the right time to buy? Timing is a huge part of investing. Stock values rise and fall all the time. You want to buy at a time of maximum potential room for growth. What you don't want to do is buy when a stock is really high and approaching its peak as you would likely soon be forced to sell for a lower value. Think of it like this, when you are at the bottom of a hill, the only way to go is up, when you are at the top of a hill, the only way to go is down. Obviously, this isn't always the case, and you shouldn't rely on timing the market, but instead try to invest for long-term growth over numerous years; however, by sometimes taking timing into account you can maximize the amount of money you make (like those who had cash and were able to buy top-quality stocks at bargain prices in March-April 2020). Young people have one major advantage when investing; they can play the "long game." This means they have many years ahead of them for their investments to grow and not worry about short-term dips.

LESSON 26
What Can You Do to Start Investing?

So now you must be wondering: Noah, what can you do to start investing if you are still a teenager?

To start with, you could open a savings account (this can be done at any age). Interest rates tend to be quite low for savings accounts (especially in recent years), but they offer a secure place to keep your money and sometimes free services for kids' accounts (such as a limited number of debits and e-transfers). Speak to a banker to understand all the terms and fees of any account before you open it. You won't beat inflation devaluing your money with the small amount of interest earned in a savings account, so the next step is to explore the investment options available to you.

If you are below the age of majority (usually 18 or 19, depending on where you live), you may need to ask your parents to buy stocks and hold them for you in their name and ask them to transfer the stocks to you when you reach the age of majority. It is important to note that the stocks would be legally owned by your parents and that they may have to pay taxes at their tax rate if the stock value increases and/or any dividends are paid.

Another option that may be available to you, depending on where you live, is an investment account for minors. Some banks will allow you to have an adult you trust co-sign for the account and help oversee your investment decisions. Once you are old enough, the adult is removed from the account and you gain full independence. It varies bank to bank, but my investment firm requires you to be at least the age of 16 to open this type of account.

In Canada there are also parent-trust investment accounts available for minors (where minors are the legal beneficiary of the investments). However, tax-filing requirements have recently changed, making accounting fees extremely high for parent-trusts and probably not worth it, especially if you don't have much money invested.

For more investment options be sure to read Lesson 29, which describes different tax-sheltered savings and investment accounts to also consider.

I highly suggest that you speak to a professional financial advisor to understand the investment and banking options available to you (which will vary depending on your age, and the laws of where you live). It is worth the effort to understand the fees involved and major tax implications. An initial consultation should be offered for free and it is well worth exploring and learning from the experts.

There is so much more I could go on about, some people dedicate their entire lives to learning about investing, but I wouldn't want to bore my poor readers. If you want to learn more, I recommend reading books specifically on investing, talking to people, and learning from your own experiences.

Chapter Five

TAXES

LESSON 27
What Are Taxes?

First off, what are taxes? Well I'm glad you asked. Taxes are how a government gets money to run public services. For any country to be safe, run smoothly, and have public services such as healthcare, roads, and libraries, we need taxes. It costs hundreds of billions of dollars a year to run Canada. And the government doesn't just pull that money out of thin air. Compared with the United States, Canada has fairly high taxes, which pays for services that benefit many Canadians. In the United States, healthcare is mostly private and costs people money, whereas in Canada it's publicly funded. This can make a big difference to a family that might otherwise go into debt to pay the high costs of healthcare. Public libraries, schools, the military forces, national parks, and road construction are all made possible due to money collected from taxes.

The government collects tax in several ways. The biggest source is through income tax. When you have a real job with a paycheque, the government takes a portion of your earnings. To redistribute wealth and keep it fair, there are several tax brackets. Depending on your earnings, you will pay more or less taxes. In 2020 the first bracket of Canadian federal income tax rates was 15% on your first $48,535 of taxable income. The next bracket is 20.5% for the next $48,535 you earn. If you made $60,000, taxes would be calculated at 15% on the first $48,535 ($7,280.25) and 20.5% on the next $11,465 ($2,350.33) for total tax of $9,630.58. It keeps going on and on, with the third bracket having 26% on the next $53,404, and then 29% on the $63,895, and lastly 33% of everything over $214,368. Whether you earn $500,000 or $20,000,000, the portion above $214,368 is taxed at the same 33% rate. This model differs from country to country, but many use a similar approach.

Another form of tax is sales tax. When you go to the store and buy something, you see the price of the item. When you actually go to purchase it, the cost is a bit more; this is because of sales tax. In most parts of Canada, sales tax is between 5% and 15%. For example, in Ontario sales tax is 13%, so when you go to buy a $1 pack of gum you actually end up paying $1.13. This is the other main way the government makes money, through your spending.

LESSON 28
Tax Brackets

When you have a part-time job as a teenager, chances are you will be in the first tax bracket. It changes every year, but many governments allow people to earn a certain amount without paying taxes at all. In Canada, tax credits reduce the calculated tax amount that we discussed in the last section. In 2020, tax credits mean that Canadians could earn $13,229 tax-free. For the most part, we teenagers probably won't be making that much anyway. For jobs where you are paid a hourly wage (such as working as a waiter or at a grocery store) but don't work enough hours a year to make more than the non-taxable amount, you can get tax refunds at the end of the year for the taxes on your earnings since employers typically take it out of your paycheque anyway. So, for the most part, while you are young you won't encounter or even need to deal with taxes. However, it's important to know for the future how tax works, especially the ways to minimize it.

Like me, many kids earn money from side jobs and earn below the annual total that would be taxable. They are not required to file income tax in Canada, but may want to for reasons we'll discuss later. However, if they are earning enough on investment income to increase earnings to above the non-taxable bracket they will need to file.

Pay close attention to this next part. When you are growing your money through investing, you are taxed on half of your gains. Imagine if you were to invest $1,000, and over a few years it doubles. You now have $2,000 and think that it's a reasonable time to cash out. You sell your shares and make $1,000. Now don't get too excited. You still have to pay taxes on your gains. The good news is that many governments want to encourage investing, so they tax capital gains at lower rates than other income, thank goodness! Currently in Canada, they include only 50% of capital gains as income that they calculate tax on at the rate for your tax bracket. So of the $1,000 that you made you would be taxed only on $500. Where I live, the maximum combined provincial and federal income tax rate was 53.5% in 2020. So the very highest possible rate you'd pay on capital gains would be 50% of that, or under 27%. If you are under the top bracket, which for the most part teenagers are, you would be paying even less tax.

Say you were in a tax bracket of 20%. Do the math. You would then need to pay 20% of 50%, which is 10% of your total gains. These percentages can still have a big impact on your gains from investments. Say you were a lawyer, earning $250,000 a year, and in the highest tax bracket (50%). If you made $1,000 from an investment, $500 of that $1,000 would be taxed and you would lose $250. That may not sound too bad, but imagine if that thousand gain was actually a million. All of a sudden, instead of bringing home a million dollars, you would be left with only $750,000. You would lose $250,000 in taxes, which would hit you a lot harder. Even though it may seem unfair, capital gains tax is a part of life. There's no getting around it—at least legally (except for a few tax savings plans that I describe below). And for those who do shady things to get around it, they can end up paying huge fines and spending time in prison with federal charges. You just have to accept that taxes exists and keep it in mind when planning your investments.

LESSON 29
Financial Tools to Help You Minimize Taxes and Increase Your Gains

This lesson might bore you, and the fact is that, unfortunately, it probably will. However, the information that we go over is so important in saving money. These tools will save the average person thousands of dollars (maybe millions) over a lifetime, and it is key to take advantage of them. I encourage you to push through and make note of the information here.

Thankfully in most countries there are ways to help minimize the taxes you pay on employment and investment income to save for emergencies, retirement, and education. In Canada, we have TFSAs, RRSPs, and RESPs. These are all financial aids and support that the Canadian government gives to encourage people to save money. Other countries have similar plans (e.g., in the US they have 401-K, IRA, and 529 plans). In one way or another, these strategies allow you to save money and minimize the amount of taxes you pay—up to a certain limit, or no one would pay any tax! As an example, let's start with TFSAs.

A TFSA (Tax-Free Savings Account) is an account provided by the Canadian government to grow your money free of taxes. However, there are a few rules and regulations. To open a TFSA you must be at least 18 years old; this means it is not an option (yet) for many of us, but it will be soon. A TFSA is an account where investment income earned on money in the account isn't reduced by income taxes. As of 2020, the annual contribution limit is $6,000. The good news is that once you have opened an account, the amount you can contribute is rolled over to the next year. So say you are unable to put any money in the first year. The next year you would have an extra $6,000 of room from the past year. TFSAs offer two main advantages: You can put money into the account, and the money that grows in that account (i.e., the income from investing the money) is not taxed even after you take it out (savings #1), as you invest your money within a TFSA, growth in your investment's value (capital gains, dividends, interest income) is also not taxed (savings #2). So as soon as you turn 18, open up a TFSA. That is where all of your savings should go until you have reached the contribution limit. Not doing so would basically be giving up free money, giving the government taxes that you don't need to pay. If you feel like it, ask your parents about their savings. Do they have a TFSA? Odds are they do, but if they don't, get them to read this book. They might need to learn a thing or two.

The next account that we will go into very briefly is an RRSP account, or a Registered Retirement Savings Plan, which is another savings and investing account in Canada that helps to defer taxes (in the US, an IRA is similar although details will differ). This account is meant particularly to be an aid in saving for retirement. The greatest advantage of an RRSP is that there is no age limit to when you can open an account. As young as you may be, you can open an RRSP account. The only problem is that there is a maximum of an 18% contribution of before-tax earned dollars from the previous year, up to an overall maximum of $27,830 in 2021. So if you make $1,000,000 in a year, you can add only $27,830 to your RRSP account and not $180,000. For most teens that isn't a problem. Most of us aren't making enough to add $27,830. An advantage for those who are earning more money, and are in higher taxable incomes, is the amount that they deposit to an RRSP each year is deducted from their taxable income (from employment and other investments), reducing the tax they have to pay that year. When you decide to take out your money from the account, the amount you withdraw is taxed at the rate of your current income. This is to encourage people to take out their cash after they've retired. For the most part, people will be in a higher tax bracket when they were working than when they retire. When retired, you might be earning money through your investments (hopefully you are, otherwise you might be in a bad situation), but odds are you're not making as much as when you were working and had a salary, so you're in a lower tax bracket and pay less taxes.

Note: You must file an income tax return with the government in order to create RRSP contribution room. Don't worry, you don't need to hire an expensive accountant for this. You can do it yourself (especially since you are young and your income is likely simple), and it may even be a good learning experience for you! You can find instructions on the Government of Canada website. Filing an income tax return is an important consideration for kids and teens who often earn cash from odd jobs. Many kids in this situation do not file income tax returns because they are well below the $13,229 limit and would not be required to pay any taxes (the limit varies every year and may be different depending on where you live). However, keeping track of your income (through paper receipts or electronically) and filing income tax returns may be well worth the effort. It will create RRSP room, which has tax savings advantages for the future. This is a good way to start investing in a tax-sheltered way before you are old enough to open a TFSA.

The third and final Canadian account that we will cover is the RESP (Registered Education Savings Plan). For us teens, this is no doubt the most important plan. The RESP is just what the name suggests. It's an account designed to help save for college, university or other post-secondary education. Just like an RRSP, earnings and growth within an RESP aren't taxed until taken out. There are different types of RESPs, but they are generally pretty similar. Most plans allow you to put money in whenever you want, but with a maximum of $50,000 per kid. For kids under seventeen, the government will also contribute some money for the account. Depending on the plan, you can either have the money invested for you or invest it yourself. The kid can access the money once they are enrolled in university, college, or other post-secondary institution. If you are planning on attending any sort of post-secondary education, an RESP is a really good strategy. Many parents (if they can afford to) will open one when their child is born. Otherwise, if they haven't, talk to them about it, and encourage them to do so. Look into government grants and support for your RESP; they can be a big help. The Canadian government currently offers grants (up to $7,200) where they match a certain percent of your RESP contributions—free money is always a bonus! If your parents aren't able to maximize contributions, you should consider transferring your own savings into an RESP account if you plan to pursue post-secondary education. Investing in an RESP allows access to free money from the government, is a tax shelter, and will help reduce your debt load in college/university—a win, win, win in my opinion.

Now the question may sometimes arise: Do I put my money in this account or that one? Well, if you are saving that money for education, the answer is obvious. RESPs are the only plan where the government will contribute for education. Most kids wouldn't be thinking about the other two options (TFSAs or RRSPs). However, whether you are thinking about them or not, it's still good to know about them for the future. After you contribute to an RESP, I would suggest you to put your money into a TFSA. This is for a few reasons: One, before you start earning higher income and paying taxes at high rates, you can save some money where its growth is not taxed along the way, and two, the resulting higher cash balance is not taxed when you withdraw it to spend. In an RRSP, high income earners can save tax when they put money in, but it is taxed when you take it out. With a TFSA there is no tax period. Not when you put your money in, not on investment growth along the way, and not when you take it out. When you're old enough (18+), everything you are saving should be put into a TFSA. The only reason I can think of that you wouldn't do so is if you are in a position where you are saving more than just the TFSA contribution limit. If you were, that would be an appropriate time to start adding to your RRSP.

Example

Like the previous example, I will illustrate these concepts with a short story of two brothers. Jack and Aiden are each twenty-five years old. Jack just graduated from college and started working as an electrician. Aiden finished a degree in kinesiology and was hired to be a trainer for the Toronto Raptors. Although working completely different jobs, both Aiden and Jack earn the same annual salary: $80,000 (before tax). Coincidentally, they also have very similar spending and saving habits, as you will come to see. Both Aiden and Jack have no kids, no debt, and not many expenses to cover. All of their living expenses, including wants, vacations, and such, cost them $52,000 a year. Both Aiden and Jack plan out their expenses for the year and make sure they have the money available for when they need it. As similar as these brothers seem, there is a slight difference that will alter the courses of their financial success. Jack has always been smart with his money and has researched and learned a lot on the topic of personal finance. He knows all about plans such as TFSAs and RRSPs and takes full advantage of them. Aiden on the other hand hasn't really ever been into personal finance and has never bothered to do a bit of learning on the topic. He does invest his money, but only in index funds that his brother Jack tells him about. Jack deposits his entire limit in his TFSA every year. As he earns money he puts it there until the annual limit of $6,000 is reached. From his $80,000 income he gets to deduct $2,500 for his RRSP contribution, leaving $77,500 taxable income. With other standard tax credits, he is left after income taxes with just under $61,000 to cover his $6,000 TFSA contribution, $2,500 RRSP contribution, and his $52,000 living expenses. His brother Aiden saves money only after all his earnings have been taxed—after provincial and federal taxes and CPP (Canada Pension Plan) and EI (Employment Insurance) deductions have been taken—he is left with about $59,580. Again, both brothers spend $52,000 a year, which leaves Aiden with $7,580 ($59,580 − $52,000) left to save. Already you can see a big difference in how much is saved between the brothers; Jack with $8,500 (from his TFSA and RRSP savings) and his poor brother Aiden with $7,580. Over 20 years that $1,000 difference would be $20,000. If they were to start investing that money, and with the power of compound growth, the gap would grow even wider as Aiden's growth is taxed every year and Jack's is tax-free.

Caution: I'm not a tax expert, but have done my best in this chapter to explain some ways to avoid paying more tax than you need to. Tax rules and rates change from year to year, so you should always check current regulations and seek expert advice if you are investing amounts that are significant to you.

Chapter Six

CREDIT CARDS AND DEBT

LESSON 30
An Introduction to Debt

First off, what is debt? Debt is a sum of money that is owed for the purchase of services or goods; that is, financial debt. Many people at some point in their lives will need to borrow money. It's inevitable. Yes, some may be born into a rich family and can have all of their expenses covered; however, for most of us that just isn't the case. Some necessities in life are very costly, and sometimes you don't have the money at the time to buy them. When people borrow money, the person or institution such as a bank, credit union, or finance company does not normally loan money for free. They charge a percentage of the amount borrowed to repay at once or over a scheduled period of time. Have you ever heard of $1,000 loans for $100? That's what I'm talking about. Whenever you borrow money, you end up paying extra for it. So, as discussed in chapter four about how you can *earn* interest off investments, in this case you *pay* interest on a loan. When people decide whether to borrow money or not, they have to think about how much it will end up costing them over the time it takes to pay off the loan. For example, if you took out a $10,000 loan, for whatever reason, you would pay interest on it as you pay it off. For example, if you had a 10% *annual* interest rate on that ten grand you'd borrowed, and you paid it back in one year, you would end up paying $10,000 × 10%, which is $1,000, plus repaying the $10,000 borrowed for a total of $11,000 in payments. However, if it took you two years to pay it off, you would also end up paying 10% of the $11,000 you owed for one year, which means you would owe $12,100. So you see, as compound interest is wonderful and amazing when it comes to growing your invested money, it can murder your finances when it comes to borrowing and owing money.

In these next pages we are going to talk about all sorts of loans and debts, from those that you might encounter in the future when you're an adult, such as mortgages and car loans, to stuff that teenagers may have to deal with daily, such as credit cards, and as they get a little older, student loans for post-secondary education such as college or university.

LESSON 31
Mortgages (Buying Property)

A common example of taking on debt is when people buy a house. Buying a home is a milestone in many people's lives.

It is also the largest single investment that most people will ever make. Many "starter" homes can cost upwards of $300,000! That's a lot of money, and that's not even a super-expensive house. According to the Canadian Real Estate Association, in 2021 the average house in Canada costs over $716,000.[1] According to Statistics Canada, in 2019 the average Canadian income was $62,900.[2] That means the average person earning sixty grand is buying a $700,000 house. Do the math. It would take over eleven years of saving only, never mind taxes and any other bills. Now that just isn't realistic. A large portion of that money goes to taxes and even more to necessities such as rent, clothes, and food. This is why many Canadians go into debt when buying homes. In normal times, houses are usually appreciating assets (grow in value), so it is totally fine to get a mortgage, which is a secured loan for a house and property. You just have to be smart and know what you can afford and what you can't.

When you reach this stage of life it can be very helpful to meet with a financial planner who can help you model how much money you will need for retirement and how much you can afford to pay for a house based on your income and spending. This is often a free service that banks and investment firms provide and is well worth exploring.

A mortgage is something that practically everyone who buys property or real estate will have to take out. By law in many countries, to be able to buy a house you have to be able to put down a minimum down payment. A down payment is a chunk of the total cost of the house that you pay in cash. The Canadian government currently requires that everyone who purchases a home makes a minimum down payment of at least 5% for homes under $500,000. That would be $25,000. So to take out a mortgage for a house costing $500,000, you would need to have $25,000 in your bank account to put down for the house. For any house over $500,000 but less than $1 million, you need to pay 5% of the first $500,000 and 10% of anything over that. For homes over $1 million you need to pay 20% for the down payment.

Now in some cases, people want to buy a home for which they can't afford the down payment. In these cases they might take out a second mortgage. A second mortgage is a mortgage on the down payment of the first mortgage. It may sound complicated, but all you're really doing is taking on a debt to pay the down payment. Second mortgages have much higher interest rates and in most cases are very, very difficult to pay off and generally are not a good idea.

Many Canadians have got themselves into too much debt due to their mortgages. This can lead to a lot of unpleasantness, from stress and anxiety about the bills to having to work several more years than others before they can afford to retire. To be fair, this may be worth it for some people. A home is one of the most important aspects of your life. You live there. And I guess for some people it's worth getting into excessive debt to have their dream home. However, as I mentioned in chapter one, studies have proven that people who live within their means are much happier and have less stress and anxiety. When buying your house in twenty years or so, take this into consideration. Live within your means and be smart about your purchases.

However, when buying a home to live in, either on your own or with your family, the most important consideration is whether or not you can afford it. Unfortunately, many Canadians purchase homes that they aren't able to afford. They take out a mortgage and sometimes a second mortgage if they get into trouble trying to pay off the house. Lenders such as banks usually require automatic payment of monthly mortgage payments from your bank account *before* you get to spend money on other stuff, even necessities such as food, so you need to carefully plan what you can afford. Mortgages are something that almost everyone will have to deal with; however, you should make sure that you have a solid down payment (the money that you pay straight up) and plan out when and how you are going to pay off your debt. There are lots of mortgage calculators online that can help you with this.

Even though your house will likely be the biggest investment you ever make, it is not something you can depend on making money from. When you grow up you will need a house for shelter. If you sell your house when the market is hot, you will most likely need to buy into the same expensive market to ensure that you still have shelter. It is true that real estate values tend to go up, but often not much more than inflation over a long period of time. Even downsizing to retirement residences can be surprisingly costly, so I suggest not depending on selling your house as a retirement investment plan and use other options that we have discussed. Make sure that you can afford the house that you buy *and* still be able save enough for retirement. Again, I highly suggest talking to a financial advisor to help with this type of planning.

LESSON 32
Again—Beware of Credit Cards

The next kind of debt that we will talk about is credit cards. We already briefly discussed them in chapter one, but now we'll explore deeper into the little chip on a card that millions of Canadians carry in their pockets every day. Credit cards are a leading cause of financial destruction among Canadians. When I say that, I mean that they cause lots and lots of financial trouble and insecurity to those who use them foolishly. Credit cards, as you already know, have very high interest rates. Many between 18% and 20%. There is no way you ever want to be in a situation where you can't fully pay off your monthly credit card bill. As you will soon learn, there are much more conservative and lower-interest forms of borrowing money. Unfortunately, as obvious as all this may be, credit cards have one benefit that many other forms of borrowing don't—convenience. With just a tap of the card you can borrow money to buy something that you otherwise might not be able to afford. Someone working for a credit card company might say something like this to support their product: "Yes, credit cards have put many Canadians into financial trouble, but they offer great convenience." When I hear that, I think to myself, hmmm, you're getting close but you're not quite there. Switch one little word in that sentence and it puts it all in a whole other light: "Yes, credit cards have put many Canadians into financial trouble, *because* they offer great convenience." — David Chilton, *The Wealthy Barber*.

If you are still young but wish to have the convenience of carrying a card around that you can use to buy things without carrying around a bunch of cash, then a debit card is a good first step. A debit card only gives you access to your own money, making you unable to get into debt (unless you have an overdraft option on your account; see Lesson 36). You can buy only what you can afford (or at least have enough money for; having the money and affording something aren't always the same thing), and you still have the convenience of the card. However, you still have to be careful and always know how much money you have in your account to keep track of your spending and to make decisions about your future spending.

I myself don't have a debit card because all my money is in cash or invested. I always keep a bit of money in my wallet in case I do wish to buy something, but for the most part I spend little and invest most of my money, making it unnecessary to have a debit card. This will likely change as I get older, move out of my parents' house, and start paying all my bills myself, but for the time being I remain without a card of any kind.

Back to the convenience of credit cards. The reason people use them so much is that they are convenient. Just tap and go. You don't even use your own money. And guess what! You have to pay only a minimum amount. Just kidding—sorry; I hope you didn't get too excited. Credit card companies are worth billions of dollars, and they didn't just magically acquire all of that money either. Yes, a portion of their earnings is made through the small transaction fee they charge. When a company accepts a credit card as payment, they give a portion of the money to the credit card company. But a very large chunk of the credit card companies' earnings is from people paying interest on their "unpaid balance"—meaning money that is owed.

LESSON 33
Using a Credit Card as a Teen

When it comes to credit cards, stay away from them at least until you have finished high school. What most kids (and unfortunately a lot of adults too) don't understand, or at least don't think about, is the fact that if you can't afford an item now, you won't be able to in the near future either. If you're buying that new phone on a credit card because you don't have $829 lying around, it's not as if you'll have the money immediately after you put it on your credit card. Say you pull together some cash and are able to pay the monthly minimum payments on each bill. Some credit card companies make you pay a percentage, usually 1% to 3% each month, or they use a set percentage. For this example we are going to say that your minimum payment is $15 a month. Say you decided to pay just the minimum payments. I suspect that anyone deciding to do something this foolish would think to themselves something like this: "Oh great, I can just pay the minimum payments and then I won't have to worry about bills, and it will all be paid off in no time!" Great, right? No, not so fast. If you were to pay the minimum payments, this is what it would look like: It would take you a grand total of 133 months to pay it off completely. Now I'm not a math genius, but that's a lot of months, and with the added interest on the unpaid balance ... Uh oh, this is going to get messy. As we discussed in Lesson 32, credit cards can charge between 18% and 20% APR (annual percentage rate), give or take. For this example we'll use 19% as a realistic amount that you'll be paying on your card's balance. After those 133 months—eleven whole years—you would have ended up paying $1,986! As I said before, I'm no mathematician, but that seems like a lot more than $829 to me. In fact, let me just pull out my calculator ... that would be $1,157 more than if you had saved a little and bought the phone in cash. By making just the minimum payments, you end up paying more than double the actual cost of the phone.

In conclusion, as a teen it is best to avoid credit cards, just wait a little bit longer to buy whatever it is that you want. Cut a few more lawns, work a few more hours at your part-time job, reschedule your birthday for a few months earlier, whatever it takes, just don't use credit to buy something you can't afford. Whenever you go to pay for that candy at the convenience store, the new shoes at Foot Locker, or the pizza for you and your friends, shove that credit card away and just use cash. There will be times when you might not be able to afford what you really want, but as the song goes, *you can't always get what you want*—or something like that. Just to make it clear, what I've been talking about is what you can spend *after* you've paid yourself first. That is by far the most important bill; don't cut out from that to buy your new Xbox or whatever major purchase you want. Just make a plan, go out, earn some extra money, and then buy it. It's really as easy as it sounds.

LESSON 34
Your Credit Score

One of the most important things to think about while dealing with credit cards is your credit score. A credit score is a rating on how reliably you pay off your bills. This score determines how much interest you pay and whether companies are willing to lend you money. The worse the rating (meaning the more unreliable you are), the higher the interest credit card companies and banks will charge to lend you money. Someone who has a record of not always paying off their loans is a risk to banks and credit companies. These companies want to make sure they are getting paid more for the extra risk. It's the same as the way insurance companies charge someone who smokes more for life insurance than someone who's healthy and doesn't smoke. When you have a credit card, the company keeps track of how reliable you are at paying off your bills on time. Your payment history is used to build your "credit score" and is shared with other companies. It will have a huge impact on your ability to borrow money for a car or a house, and even on smaller things such as signing a cellphone plan contract.

A common trouble that teens and young adults sometimes get themselves into is the destruction of their score. For these people it's due to a combination of irresponsible spending habits and their high costs with little earnings as a student. This is especially common for university students. Some university students foolishly rely on their credit cards for all their loans. As I mentioned earlier, this is a very, very bad idea. With extremely high interest rates and the significant risk of damaging your credit score, credit cards are not a good borrowing option, except for short-term convenience—*only if* you have the ability and discipline to pay the entire balance owed on time every month. Teenagers and young adults sometimes fail to make a few payments, which can really start to hurt their credit scores. A poor credit score is difficult to turn around. With a damaged credit score you will be stuck paying much higher interest rates than necessary, and may not qualify for loans at all.

And higher interest rates aren't even the worst of it. When applying for bigger loans (and sometimes especially meaningful ones), if you have a poor credit rating you can be turned away. Imagine how frustrating it would be to apply for a mortgage that you *can* afford, and then being refused or rejected because of mistakes you made in the past. When applying for other loans such as lines of credit, which we'll talk about in Lesson 38, a poor credit rating can limit the amount that you can take out, if any at all if the rating is really bad. With credit cards there is a maximum amount of credit that you are allowed to use; it can be set up daily, weekly, or even monthly. Having a poor credit rating will make your maximum amount smaller. All of this could be very difficult and frustrating.

However, one of the advantages of having a credit card is to be listed with a (hopefully) good credit rating by paying monthly the balance owed in full and on time. When applying for other types of credit and loans without a credit card and a credit score, you may not be able to take advantage of the lowest interest rates. Therefore, I would recommend the use of a credit card only when you are old enough to be responsible for payments.

My nana has a very good credit rating due to her history of always paying off her debts on time. A few years ago she was on vacation and completely forgot about her monthly credit card bill. She missed the payments and was consequently charged a lot of extra interest as a penalty. Fortunately, this was the first time this had ever happened to her and when she called the credit card company and explained the situation, they were very understanding. Due to this being the first time my nana had ever missed a payment, they let her off the hook with no charge. Her credit score wasn't affected and she didn't have to pay the fees. This real-life example just goes to show how beneficial it is to maintain a good credit score.

Invest? Or Pay Off Debt?

In the next few lessons we will discuss other forms of loans and credit, but to side track a bit, I want to bring in another idea. Some people, when they have money saved up, will have to decide what to do with it. Do they invest? Or do they pay off a loan such as their mortgage for example? First off, this is a pretty good problem to have, but when looking at what to actually do with the money there is a fairly simple resolution. With a loan you lose money. With an investment you make money. By cutting back on how much you owe you are making money. When growing your money you are also making money. Now you have to look at one thing. The interest. Whichever choice has a higher interest rate, that's the one you should go for. Say your loan costs you 12% a year, and you make on average 8% from your investments, then you would obviously choose to pay off the loan. I personally would rather not pay 12% and make nothing, than make 8% and pay 12%. There may be rare occasions when you think you can make more off an investment, but for the most part paying off loans is the better idea. Investing is risky; there is a chance you might not make the money you expect to make. Loans are much more predictable; once you've paid them off you are no longer in debt and no longer being charged interest.

Aside from the financial point of view, paying off any loans is much better for your mental wellbeing. Whenever I owe someone money, whether it's my parents or a friend, I always pay it off right away before spending it on anything else—I guess I just don't like the feeling of owing someone money. There are studies that support my thinking. Surveys and studies have shown that people with no debt are on average happier and more content with their lives than your average debt carrier. So whenever you owe your friend for that lunch, or your parents for that new pair of shoes, just go out and do it. Pay off the debt! Trust me, you will feel a lot better—not only mentally but financially as well—especially if whomever you owe is charging you interest. Just Pay It! The longer you wait the more it will cost you. Whether buying with credit or cash, stuff costs money, and with credit it ends up costing a lot more.

LESSON 36
Overdraft

The next kind of debt we'll discuss is overdraft. Overdraft is probably the simplest form of debt. It's when you spend more than you have in your bank account. There are two types of overdraft: authorized and unauthorized. An authorized overdraft is what it sounds like, you have an agreement with your bank to draw from your account a certain amount more than what you have in your account, thus taking on a debt. An unauthorized overdraft is just the opposite, it's either when you have no agreement with your bank or if you do have an agreement and you spend more than your overdraft limit. An overdraft allows you to continue spending money from your account even when it's balance is at zero. It is like any other loan, once you use the extra credit you've been given, you're charged interest fees and sometimes other fees. However good this may seem, the interest fees are quite high, around 22% annually. This makes it unsuitable for any sort of long-term borrowing. And if you ever find yourself in a position where you are overdrawn, you have some serious financial problems that need to be mended as quickly as possible.

LESSON 37
Be Wary of Loaning to Friends

I would advise you never to lend to or borrow from friends. There's an old saying: "Don't do business with friends." It's the same with money. Due to your personal connection with a friend, you may feel inclined to lend them money when they ask for it. But let's be real here. How many of your friends would be guaranteed to pay you back all of the money? Even if they are good people and you really trust them, you don't always know what they are like with their money. Are they responsible? Are they going to be able to pay you back? You are giving them your hard-earned money here; you don't want to just hand it out for free.

Of course, spotting friends for small amounts of money is okay, and it feels good to be generous, but I advise against loaning significant amounts. It is not worth straining a friendship over finances. Good relationships with family and close friends are far more valuable over a lifetime than money. Lending a significant amount can do long-term damage if it can't be repaid quickly. Instead, help them out by sharing the valuable lessons about finances that you are learning from this book!

LESSON 38
Line of Credit (LOC)

The next type of loan that we'll talk about is a line of credit (LOC). A line of credit is a neat way of borrowing. The lender, whether it be a bank or a credit service, loans you a certain amount of money. Then once you have taken out a line of credit, it can be borrowed as needed, paid back, and borrowed again. You have a limit on the amount that you can borrow at once, but once you pay it back you still have the available credit. Say for example I get a $2,000 LOC approved at my bank; that means I have two grand of credit at my disposal. It's almost as if you have a bank account in which you have a certain amount of money, and once you take that money out you have less, and once you put more in, you have more. The only difference is that it's credit (not actually your money—you still have to pay interest and fees) and there is a limit. Say I want the newest model of AirPods, I could go into the line of credit and take out the $300 that they roughly cost. Now I have $1,700 left of credit. Once I pay off the $300 that I took out, I'm back to the maximum of $2,000. The nice thing about a line of credit is that you pay interest only on the money you've taken out. When I take out $300 for the pair of AirPods that I really want, I'm paying interest only on that $300 from the time when I take it out to when I pay it back. Depending on the line of credit, there may also be fees involved such as an administration or opening fee. Usually the interest on a LOC is fairly low— *much* lower than credit cards—and sometimes these interest rates will fluctuate over time. (Note that I am using this example to describe how a line of credit works—of course I always advocate for carefully evaluating your needs vs. wants, and I don't recommend going into to debt for unnecessary purchases.)

A few things determine how much interest you pay on your LOC. The first being your credit score. As we discussed in Lesson 34, people with a poor credit rating may have to pay higher interest rates on their loans related with their added risk. The other variable that determines how much interest you pay is whether your LOC is secured or unsecured. A secured line of credit is when you agree to have some sort of collateral (something pledged as a security for the loan if it goes unpaid); a common collateral could be something like a car or a house. If you fail to pay back what you owe, the person or company lending the money to you has the legal right to take whatever the collateral was. This can be quite scary, but if you are smart with your money you'll never have to worry about repaying loans and having collateral property seized by lenders. The other option is an unsecured loan. An unsecured loan is when there is no collateral; this means it is more risky for the bank or lender, which normally leads to your having to pay higher interest rates. "Secured" loans generally have lower interest rates, and "unsecured" have higher.

I strongly advocate living within your means as a teenager and never going into debt. Just do extra work and save until you can afford what you need (and don't forget to "pay yourself first" and invest most of your hard-earned money). On the other hand, adults who need to make a necessary purchase, such as a car, for the most part a line of credit can be a fairly good option for borrowing. Your limit and the interest that you pay depends on a few conditions. Lenders will decide based on your level of income, current debt, and your credit rating. For the most part, interest rates are much lower than those of credit cards, being as low as 3%. This is a much better option than a credit card for something that will take you some time to pay off.

Example

I have two sisters, Lilah and Adele, who really wanted to be included in this book, so I am using their names to write this purely fictional story to demonstrate an important lesson.

There are two sisters, Lilah and Adele. Both of them really, really like ponies, and each sister wants her own pony! They live in an old farmhouse with a big enough property for the ponies to live on, and both sisters are willing to do all the chores and take care of their new "pets." There is only one problem—their parents aren't going to drop the $1,500 that each of the animals cost. Lilah can't afford to spend the money to buy her pony and neither can Adele. They had to come up with another solution. Against their better financial judgement, these sisters decided that they were going to buy these ponies, and the only way for them to do so was by going into debt.

Adele, being the smarter of the two, decided to open a line of credit to purchase her pony. Lilah, on the other hand, is not the sharpest pencil in the box. Over the thirteen years of her life, she has racked up impressive credit card bills and is notorious for paying only the minimum amounts. Adele takes out a line of credit from the nearby bank. Given her excellent credit rating—from her past history of responsible spending—she receives a line of credit up to $5,000 with an interest fee on her balance of 7%. Lilah, on the other hand, is charged the annual percentage rate (APR) of 19% on her credit card. To be fair, each sister earns $4,000 a year. Adele responsibly decides that she should prioritize her debt over any other spending, including investing, considering she is not guaranteed to make over 7% each year on her investments. Lilah takes the flipside, spending almost as much as she normally does—meaning everything she earns. To her credit (no pun intended), she does manage to cut her spending just a little to pay the monthly minimum payments, 2.5% of the original balance ($37.50). The sisters' parents generously offered to pay any expenses for the ponies after the sisters had actually bought them. Adele earns around $333 a month. She dedicates $200 of that towards her debt, living frugally on $133 a month. Well not too frugally—her parents pay for all her needs, and even some of her wants. Adele follows through with her plan and ends up paying off her debt completely in eight months. Her total interest (extra money paid, not including paying off the original balance of $1,500) is a mere $38.39. Not too bad. Yes, it is extra money paid, and the ideal option would have been to save up and then pay in full. However, when borrowing this amount of money, the interest charges on the debt could be a lot worse, as we will soon see with Adele's poor sister (again no pun intended).

Lilah uses her credit card to buy the pony in one go. Just a tap of the card and boom, she got her pony. As mentioned earlier, Lilah has been known to pay only the minimum payments on her credit card. She goes about spending the usual amount that she normally does (waaay over how much she actually makes) and sets aside a small amount of money each month towards the pony bill. Just by paying the minimum payments it took her *only* five years and four months to pay off her balance. And the good news is that she had to pay *only* $895.04 in interest charges. Obviously I'm being sarcastic. Each year she was paying way more than the original cost of the pony. And Adele, who earns the same amount each year, managed to pay it off in just over eight months, whereas Lilah ended up paying $2,395.04 ($1,500 + $895.04), which was over $800 more than the $1,538.39 ($1,500 + $38.39) Adele paid.

By now you are probably thinking, "Wow, Lilah is a complete idiot." That's good because it means you learned something: Sensible people, when it comes to finance, think the same way. Sadly, thousands of Canadians, if not more, don't realize the hazards of credit card use. They make decisions just like Lilah in this fictional story. As of December 2019, Canadians had racked up $100 billion in credit card debt and have since kept adding to it.[3] In 2019 Canada's population was 37.59 million. Do the math: $100,000,000,000 ÷ 37,590,000 equals around an average per person of $2,660 in credit card debt alone. And a percentage of that 37.59 million are kids who don't have credit cards, making the debt on average even higher per credit card holder. Just the sheer amount of debt our relatively small (population-wise) country has is both eye opening and alarming. (Note: Don't tell them, but my sisters are actually both very smart with their money and have been investing their money earned from lemonade stands, babysitting, and plant sales for years!)

LESSON 39
Can Debt Be Used as an Advantage?

To end this chapter on credit cards and debt, I'd like to introduce a small idea. This may sound a bit advanced, but it's a question on some people's minds and I think it's best to bring it up here. Is there ever a time when you can use debt to your financial advantage? The answer is yes. Some of the richest people in the world love debt. When you take on a debt or credit, you have to pay a certain interest fee on the debt. Now think, what if you could get into debt and make money off it? Sometimes a situation can arise where you can make more money off an investment than you would be charged in interest on borrowing. You could then borrow to buy more shares and make a profit. If you were to earn say 40% off an investment, and you can get a line of credit for 7%, do the math: 40% − 7% = 33%, you would still be earning 33% on that investment. Obviously it's less than if you didn't use credit to buy, but it's 33% of the money that's not even yours going straight to your bank account. Say I were to borrow $2,000. I'd done research and found a stock that I was very excited about and thought I could make a lot of money in a relatively short period of time by investing in it. I take out the $2,000 and invest it in the stock. Say my predictions were correct and the stock jumped 75% from when I bought it a month ago. I sell the shares and come out with $3,500. Now I owe back $2,000 of that, plus 7% in interest charges ($2,140), which I pay back, leaving me with $1,360 (before deducting capital gains taxes), which I made off someone else's money. Say I hadn't taken out the debt, guess how much money I would be left with—that's right, zero. This is called "using leverage"; it's a tactic that many successful investors use. Leverage refers to using debt to invest in any kind of investment in the hope of making a profit.

Personally I have never done this, it is very risky and I've never found an opportunity where it could be possible. Actually, that's not necessarily true. At the time of this writing, there is a lot of going on in the world. If you are reading this, you will have lived through the 2020–2021 COVID-19 global pandemic, which has impacted the lives of billions. My school was closed in March 2020 and will likely remain shut down until the fall of 2021. It is a scary and uncertain time, and along with all this global health mayhem, the stock markets are crashing. Just after February 20, 2020, the stock markets crashed and plummeted into a recession. A recession by definition is a period of temporary economic decline during which trade and industrial activity are reduced, generally identified by a fall in the gross domestic product (GDP) in two successive quarters. In this case, it is related to the millions of unemployed workers, the shutdown of factories, and the fear and uncertainty for the future. The Canadian stock market (the Toronto Stock Exchange, or TSX) has seen the worst day since the Great Depression. To try and combat the crashing economy, the government is working on different stimulus packages. This is when they take out a loan on themselves and print more money to help the economy. The loan makes sure that rapid inflation doesn't occur and allows the government to send help packages to jobless citizens to boost the economy. All that is just a basic understanding of it, but it's all you need to know for now.

One measure the government discussed was to forgive student debt. For all of those people who still have nagging student debt, the government is repaying or forgiving it, this is hoped to boost the economy. Realistically, the average worker and citizen will feel the effects of this recession for at least the next few years. People are going to have to change the way they spend, save, and invest their money. It will be a hard time for the majority of Canadians, and that is why it is so essential that you read a book like this, find good information, and be smart with your money. Feel more than free to share this book with your parents; hopefully it will help them too.

With all of this going on, the stock market has been acting like the economy is heading into a recession. Basically, that means that the economy is in a bit of a downfall. On March 12, 2020, the Toronto Stock Exchange saw its worst day since 1940. That's eighty years ago. Due to lots of negative headlines around the coronavirus, investors started to panic. This caused the market to plunge into a bear market. A bear market is when the market is driven by fear and causes a large stock market decline. Many of the biggest companies in the world have taken substantial hits. Disney went down nearly 50%. Air Canada went down 67%, and the list goes on and on. I really wanted to take the opportunity to buy stocks when they were so low. With school out I've had lots of time on my hands. I decided that since the number of available yard-work services were down due to job restrictions during the pandemic, I would help out my neighbours and make a bit of money doing so. I followed safety protocol to help lower the risk of infection and accepted e-transfers, making no contact with my clients. In the first two weeks since school closed I'd made over $1,200 just from yard work. With the stock market down, I immediately transferred that money into my RBC investing account. I also managed to convince my parents to lend me some extra money, which I paid off quickly with earnings from some more jobs. Thankfully, my parents don't charge interest on their short-term loans to me, so it wasn't a very risky thing to do. But in a sense I was using leverage by taking on a loan to buy into a company. Even though I don't like borrowing money, I really wanted to take advantage of the dip in the market with hopes of a high return. In this case it all worked out, but it can be very risky.

The best investment I made was probably not even the buying of the stocks. Out of the nine houses I did yard work for, four of them have hired me to mow their lawns this summer. By taking the time and doing the yard work, I came out with a summer-long gig of mowing four lawns, and on average they are paying me just over $100 a week. Over the course of the summer and a bit into the fall I'll be bringing in the profits of that investment every single week.

People should be borrowing to invest only if they are in a position where they can afford to lose the money because, unlike a normal investment, you're losing someone else's money. And whether you like it or not, you will have to pay that money back plus some with interest, so you could potentially lose more than if you had invested your own money. I thought I'd add this so that if you were ever in a position someday, maybe now, maybe in the future, this could be an option. Again, it is very risky and should be taken advantage of only if you are in a situation where you can afford to lose the money.

Chapter Seven

ADVANCED LESSONS

If you have come this far, you are well on the path to financial success. Up to this point, you have a good grounding in the workings of the financial world, and you are now ready to learn some interesting and more advanced lessons. In this chapter, we will cover topics such as investing, trading, insurance, and more. Some of what you learn here will be information that you don't need to know until you are older. However, it is always good to expand your knowledge and horizons.

If you don't feel ready yet to go any further, you can trust in the knowledge and understanding that you have gained in the previous chapters, and hopefully you can begin your successful financial journey. If you feel that this isn't the right time for you to continue reading, just put the book aside and perhaps come back to it in a month, a year, or even a decade. It's up to you.

For those of you who have decided to read on, congrats, you are on your way to broadening your financial knowledge.

LESSON 40

A Brief Understanding of Risk

No one has a crystal ball to predict which companies will do well and which ones will not. This means there is some risk in investing in the stock market. Nevertheless, through educated guesses and logical thinking you can determine which companies are likely to be riskier investments than others. For example, a bank stock is much more stable and less risky than, say, a startup marijuana stock. Banks have been around for hundreds of years and always make money, in Canada anyway. Marijuana companies are new and most of them do not yet make any money. Generally, the really risky investments offer the chance to make a lot of money (at least in the short term)—but they also have a high chance of losing your money. Something like a bank stock will likely stay around and grow at a more predictable rate, although nothing is truly predictable, some ventures are more predictable than others.

One of the biggest limiters of risk is diversification. Diversification in investment terms is to have a wide variety of stocks from a number of different industries in your "portfolio" (a word for your collection of investments). Think of it like this, if you were to invest all of your money in a single industry, oil for example, then your success would depend completely on that one industry. But what would happen if everyone switched to clean electricity and abandoned oil and gas? The oil industry would take a huge hit and, consequently, so would your savings. With a portfolio having investments in a wide range of industries, if one industry were to take a big hit, the rest of your portfolio would balance out the loss. The wise old expression "don't put all your eggs in one basket" is another way of thinking about having diversified investments.

LESSON 41
Baskets of Stocks

When you are young, it's unlikely that you have a lot of money. With a limited amount of money, you likely wouldn't have enough to buy a wide variety of stocks. For example, let's say you have saved $200. Some stocks might cost $100 each. This means that you could buy two stocks of one company or one stock of two companies. The good news is that there are other investments that can help with that. You might have heard of types of investments such as mutual funds, index funds, and exchange traded funds (ETFs). These are all different financial vehicles that pool money from a lot of investors to buy a basket of stocks. This means that your $200 could be spread across many different companies.

This may sound a bit complicated, but don't worry, it isn't. Investors buy these securities and their investment joins a large pool of money from all of the other investors. Investors' shares will go up and down with the fund. Large teams of investors invest the money in different kinds of stocks; for example, one share of a mutual or index fund might be made up of pieces of a hundred different stocks. You have a small proportion of all of those stocks in your one single share. This allows you to have a more widely distributed portfolio, making your investment less risky. For the most part, less risk comes with less potential reward, but that's okay—and it's not always the case. The best investors are those who minimize risk without affecting their earnings. When investing when you're young, sometimes you will want your money to grow at a steady, reliable rate. This may be because you're saving for something like university or a down payment on a house. When buying into funds, you also need to be wary of the fees involved. The people who manage and invest these large pools of money definitely don't do it for free, just as a financial advisor or stockbroker often charges a percentage of the money you have invested. Be wary of the fees when deciding where to put your money. Find a financial advisor who can offer a wide range of products from a variety of sources. Some banks currently offer only their own products, which are usually mutual funds with high fees. Find a bank or investment firm that can offer a full range of products, including ETFs and index funds, which usually have lower fees than mutual funds.

I started out by buying index funds. Since I had only a small amount of cash to invest, I wasn't willing to bet it all on a few companies. I stayed away from any mutual funds as I found their fees to be too costly. The index funds that I bought were the Vanguard VCN and the Vanguard VFV. They performed at a good rate of growth for the years I had them. After I had earned a bit more money, I decided it was time for me to start diversifying and buying individual stocks. I bought stocks with the help of my parents' financial advisor, and believe it or not, my investing-savvy Nana. She has been quite a successful investor, and with her many years of experience, thanks to her age (just kidding, Nana, that was a joke), I always go to her for advice.

Over the past couple of years I have been growing and expanding my portfolio while still holding on to my index funds. The stocks I own now come from a wide variety of businesses, from real estate, to banks, to technology, to energy, and over time I've built quite a diverse portfolio.

LESSON 42
More Alternatives for Investments

As mentioned in Lesson 25 (page 70), there are many investment alternatives to just stocks or shares in a company. Let's start with one of the more common ones in Canada: GICs or "guaranteed investment certificates." A GIC is an account set up by banks where you put your money with the agreement to not withdraw it for a certain period of time. The banks will usually pay you a higher interest rate for this than they pay on a savings account where you can withdraw your money at any time. In recent years in Canada GICs pay around 2% to 3% interest annually. Normally the longer you agree not to touch that money the higher rate they will pay you. The reason banks are willing to do this is that they actually invest your money. Banks take all the money they have in GICs and invest it with their experts. Banks never do anything that they can't profit from. While they pay you 2% to 3% a year, your money might be making them upwards of 8%. This raises the question of whether or not GICs are the best use of your money. What if you, instead of the bank, could be making that 8%? Not only would your money grow by more, but you might also be able to liquidate and access the cash whenever you needed it. However, this does take time, risk, and learning, but if you could be earning four times more from of your investments, why not spend the time, take the risk, and start learning? No one gets rich off of GICs; however, many do get rich off the stock market. I'm not saying go put all your money in penny stocks and cross your fingers for good luck. No, what I'm saying is follow the lessons and guidelines in this book and make smart decisions. Even if you mess up now, you're still young—a much better time to lose a bit of money and learn from the mistakes than when you are an adult and might need it. Many investors have a balance of investments such as GICs *and* stocks.

Another type of investment, probably the riskiest, but with the potential highest payoff, is company ownership. When entrepreneurs are starting up a new company, they will pour everything into it. Many of these men and women are betting everything on the future of their company. Those who are already successful business people might be pooling money from other investors to help out, but for the most part, the founders require everything they have to get started. This can be a very risky investment because if the company were to tank so would all of your money. However, such an investment can be profitable and successful. From Jeff Bezos to Elon Musk, the majority of the richest people in the world made the most of their fortune through entrepreneurship. By owning the entirety, or at least a large chunk, of a company from the beginning, you can profit greatly off your stake once the company grows. However, it is worth mentioning that many businesses fail, which means the owners lose their money.

LESSON 43
Online Investing Games

If you are just stepping into the world of investing and aren't yet feeling confident enough to invest your own money, don't stress it. There are all sorts of online tools and games that allow you to practise investing with fake money. Sites such as Investopedia and MarketWatch Virtual Stock Exchange allow users to "invest" and trade fake money in the stock market. You can follow how well the stocks perform that you chose to buy and the money you would have made or lost doing so. It can be fun to bet fake money on stocks and see how you do. These games can teach you a lot of valuable lessons and give you experience before you start investing your hard-earned real money. They allow you to see what your good investments were and which ones you blew your money on.

Although investing games can be fun, I would also strongly encourage everyone to actually start investing their real-life money as soon as they feel ready. The effects of starting as early as possible will help you in the future. You don't have to take on a lot of risk—although, since you're young, it's the best time to make mistakes and experiment—just do some research and talk to people. Maybe your parents have a financial advisor, or maybe they even invest themselves. In my experience parents, grandparents, or other adults in your life can be a great source of knowledge and learning; they're older, have been through more, and have tons of lessons and experience to share. Talk to people you know; talk to your friends—anyone who invests their money. You can also start to do the research yourself. Start or join an investment club; although I've never been in one I know quite a few people who have, and it sounds as though these clubs can be really helpful. Other people's experiences, mistakes, and lessons can help you develop your own road towards success. The bottom line is to start making something productive happen with your money, and the earlier you start doing this, the better.

LESSON 44
Make the World a Better Place

One way to make the world a better place is to invest in what you believe in, not in what you disagree with. For example, you may not want to invest in companies that pollute; build weapons; or promote smoking, vaping, or marijuana use. You can choose companies that develop renewable energy, promote sustainability and health, and are overall better for humanity or our planet. Not only will you be doing the right thing, but you will also likely be making more sound financial choices rather than investing in volatile markets such as marijuana companies that claim to be "organic," but are then found to be using toxic illegal pesticides (this is a real-life example), or companies that are filling our oceans with plastic and our atmosphere with greenhouse gases.

To make things simple, there are ethical index funds that you can invest in (but in this case you allow the fund manager to decide on what is deemed "ethical"), or you can research companies and make your own choices regarding what ethical values are important to you. Ethical investing is becoming more popular, and there are even firms that specialize in it. Decide what kind of world you want to live in and then support companies that share these values.

EPILOGUE

Congratulations, you have read through the entire book, or maybe you just skipped to the end. Anyway, I thank you for reading this book and wish you the best in all your future financial endeavours. Don't worry if you haven't made the smartest financial decisions in the past; the best time to start saving was when you earned your first dollar, but the second-best time is now. Remember, start early, save first, be creative, find new ways to make money, live within your means, beware of targeted advertising, and find happiness in non-material things. I wish you success in all aspects of your life.

Take care,
Noah

GLOSSARY

bear market: A period of falling stock prices, typically by 20% or more. During a bear market, investors become negative and many people sell their shares of stock in the hope of avoiding further loses.

capital gains: The profit made through the sale of an investment that has grown in value.

capital loss: The loss made through the sale of an investment that had declined in value.

chequing account: A deposit account at a bank that allows withdrawals and deposits. It is easy to access your money with these accounts through cheques, ATM machines, debit cards, online banking, and other methods.

commodities: A raw material such as gold, oil, wheat or coffee that can be bought and sold and invested in.

compound growth: The process in which the increase in an investment's value (through capital gains, dividends, interest, etc.) is kept or re-invested to earn additional value growth on the increased amount as well as on the original money invested over time. See *compound interest* for the simplest case of this.

compound interest: The process in which interest earned on an investment is reinvested and earns additional interest over a period of time.

cost-value analysis; aka cost-benefit analysis: Measuring the cost vs. the benefit of a purchase in order to decide if the benefit outweighs the price. Known risks are usually factored into this analysis.

credit rating: An assessment of a potential borrower's income and history with credit, debt, and other financial obligations to estimate their ability and likelihood to make required payments to receive a loan.

credit score: A number between 300 and 850 that rates a consumer's probability of repaying the loan in a timely manner. The higher the score the more reliable the borrower and the more appealing and lower risk they are to potential lenders. The score is based on a person's past financial history.

currencies: A system of money in general use in a country.

debit card: A card issued by the bank that allows the holder to transfer money electronically from their account to other bank accounts when making a purchase.

debt: Money borrowed from and owed to a lender (usually a bank).

depreciating assets: Categories or classes of assets that generally decrease in value over time.

diversification: A risk-management strategy when investing in which you divide your money among many different areas with the goal of lowering your overall risk. "Don't put all your eggs in one basket."

dividends: A specified sum of money paid regularly by a company to its shareholders from the company's profits.

down payment: A required sum of money that a buyer pays right away when making a big purchase such as a house or car, often before financing the rest of the cost with a lease, loan or mortgage.

entrepreneur: An individual who creates a new business, taking on a lot of risk but holding more of the rewards.

exchange traded fund (ETF): A type of security that invests in a sector, index, commodity, or other asset that can be bought and sold as a regularly traded security, such as a stock.

financial advisor: A qualified and accredited professional whose job is to provide financial expertise and advice for clients when making decisions about investments, personal finance, and other money matters.

guaranteed investment certificate (GIC): An investment contract from an insurance company or bank in which the lender deposits money into an account for a certain period of time (usually between one and five years) with a guaranteed interest rate on their deposit.

income tax: A tax imposed by the government on business and individual income every year to fund government expenses and public services such as education and healthcare.

index fund: A type of investment fund made to match or track certain components of a market. Due to the diversification that an index fund offers, they are typically considered a low-cost way to reduce risk and match market performance.

industry: Similar companies are grouped together into industries based on the type of work they perform. Some examples include the computer, agriculture, and education industries. Similar groupings or categories that describe companies' types of products/services; the markets where they sell them can be called "sectors" or "verticals."

inflation: The decrease in purchasing power over time. An increase in prices and a fall in the value of money. In recent decades, Canada has experienced inflation (decrease in purchasing value of its dollar) of a small percentage each year.

interest: The cost a borrower of money must pay to the lender. Usually a percentage of the money borrowed is paid at a scheduled interval.

invest: To commit money with the goal of earning a financial return.

investment advisor: An accredited and qualified person or group that gives investment recommendations and will do research for a fee.

leverage: The use of borrowed money to enable a larger investment in the hope of making greater profits. Caution: this can also result in greater losses.

line of credit: A flexible loan of money within a specified limit that allows you, for as long as you wish, to access, repay, and borrow from again within that limit.

liquidate: To convert investments, property, or other assets into cash by selling them.

mortgage: A type of loan used to buy property or a home. A mortgage gives the lender the ability to seize ownership of (repossess) the property if the borrower fails to repay the loan on time.

mutual fund: A company that pools large amounts of money from many investors to invest in a variety of stocks, bonds, and other securities for a fee. Investors in mutual funds own shares that represent a part of all the securities that the fund buys into.

overdraft: A form of debt when someone creates a deficit in their bank account by drawing more money than the account holds. Usually banks will charge high fees when the person drops below the agreed upon amount of allowed overdraft.

portfolio: A collection of financial securities such as stocks, commodities, cash, GICs, bonds, and other investments.

real rate of return: The annual profit earned on an investment adjusted for inflation. For example, if an investment earned 6% in a year but the dollar value dropped 1% due to inflation, the real rate of return is 5%.

recession: A period of economic struggle with lower volumes of trading and industrial activity. This means that there are fewer jobs, businesses and stocks do poorly, and people are making less and spending less money.

registered education savings plan (RESP): A government-sponsored program in Canada that assists with the payment for children's future post-secondary education.

return: The money made or lost from an investment.

registered retirement savings plan (RRSP): A plan provided by the government to encourage Canadian workers to save for retirement by tax deductions when deposits are made and tax-sheltering of investment income when deposited.

sales tax: A tax charged by the government on the sale of goods and services.

securities: Any investment made on tradeable or fixed-income financial assets.

shareholder: An owner of shares in a company, which represent ownership of a portion of the overall company.

startup: A new company in its first stages of operation.

stockbroker: A professional trader who will buy and sell shares on a stock exchange on behalf of their clients.

stock market: A place in which investors buy shares in a public venue. Usually stock markets are particular to companies from a certain country and are regulated by that government.

stocks: A small portion of ownership in a company that the company sells to raise money.

student debt: Debt that students take on to pay for education (usually post-secondary).

taxes: A mandatory contribution by companies and people earning money to pay for government expenditures.

tax-free savings account (TFSA): A savings account in Canada with a yearly contribution limit where your money can earn interest, dividends, and capital gains tax free.

trade: In finances, trading is the action of buying and selling assets.

tuition: A fee charged for education at a school, college, or university.

volatile: When prices move quickly in reaction to events or mood swings in the market.

NOTES

Introduction

1. CBC, "Lottery Win Is Retirement Plan for 34% of Poll Respondents," January 30, 2014, https://www.cbc.ca/news/ business/lottery-win-is-retirement-plan-for-34-of-poll-respondents-1.2517046.

2. Noah Zivitz, BNN Bloomberg, "Canadians 'Drowning in Debt' as 47% Struggle to Cover Costs," October 28, 2019, https://www. bnnbloomberg.ca/canadians-drowning-in-debt-as-47-struggle-to-cover-costs-mnp-1.1338497.

Chapter One

1. Anne Carrns, "Average Weekly Allowance? It's $30, a New Survey Finds," *New York Times*, October 4, 2019, https://www.nytimes. com/2019/10/04/your-money/weekly-allowance-average.html.

2. The Heart and Stroke Foundation of Canada, "The 2020–2021 Youth and Young Adult Vaping Project," March 24, 2021, https:// www.heartandstroke.ca/-/media/pdf-files/get-involved/yyav-full-report-final-eng-24-3-2021.ashx.

3. Jia Wertz, "How to Win Over Generation Z, Who Hold $44 Billion of Buying Power," *Forbes*, October 28, 2918, https://www.forbes.com/sites/jiawertz/2018/10/28/how-to-win-over-generation-z-who-hold-44-billion-of-buying-power/?sh=25fffd424c13.

4. Ashley Whillans, "Time for Happiness: Why the Pursuit of Money Isn't Bringing You Joy—and What Will," *Harvard Business Review*, January 29, 2019, https://www.awhillans.com/uploads/1/2/3/5/123580974/whillans_03.19.19.pdf.

5. Sabrina Helm, Joyce Serido, Sun Young Ahn, Victoria Ligon, and Soyeon Shim, "Materialist Values, Financial and Pro-environmental Behaviors, and Well-being," *Young Consumers*, July 24, 2019, https://www.emerald.com/insight/content/doi/10.1108/YC-10-2018-0867/full/html.

6. Statista Accounts, "Sales of Lotteries in Canada in 2020 (in Million Canadian Dollars), by Province or Territory," December 2020, https://www.statista.com/statistics/388346/sales-of-lotteries-by-province-canada/.

Chapter Three

1. Valérie Ouellet, "40% of Ontario Full-time Post-secondary Students Granted Free Tuition CBC Analysis Shows," CBC News, February 4, 2019, https://www.cbc.ca/news/canada/toronto/ontario-schools-tuition-data-1.5003005.

Chapter Six

1. Realestate News, "$716K Is the Average House Price in Canada. Here's What You Can Get for That," April 29, 2021, https://realestatenews24.com/716k-is-the-average-house-price-in-canada-heres-what-you-can-get-for-that/.

2. Statistics Canada, "Canadian Income Survey, 2019," March 23, 2021, https://www150.statcan.gc.ca/n1/daily-quotidien/210323/dq210323a-eng.htm.

3. Colin McClelland, "Canadians Racked Up $100 Billion in Credit Card Debt for First Time Ever and They're Not Done Adding to It," *Financial Post*, December 9, 2019, https://financialpost.com/news/economy/canadians-racked-up-100-billion-in-credit-card-debt-for-first-time-ever-and-theyre-not-done-adding-to-it.